STRONG SHOULDERS

STRONG SHOULDERS

Barry Albin-Dyer

Hodder & Stoughton
LONDON SYDNEY AUCKLAND

Text copyright © 2005 by Barry Albin-Dyer

First published in Great Britain in 2005
by Hodder & Stoughton

The right of Barry Albin-Dyer to be identified as the Author
of the Work has been asserted by him in accordance with the
Copyright, Designs and Patents Act 1988.

1

A catalogue record for this book is available from the
British Library

ISBN 0 340 86296 3

Typeset by Avon DataSet Ltd, Bidford on Avon, Warwickshire
Printed and bound in Great Britain by
Clays Ltd, St Ives plc

The paper used in this book is a natural recyclable
product made from wood grown in sustainable forests.
The hard coverboard is recycled.

Hodder & Stoughton
A Division of Hodder Headline Ltd
338 Euston Road
London NW1 3BH

www.madaboutbooks.com

This book is for all funeral directors who dedicate their lives to this honourable and excellent profession. You are all very special people.

My thanks also go to everybody working in the death-care industry. It is a true vocation – so guard it well.

CONTENTS

ACKNOWLEDGEMENTS

To the countless funeral journals from around the world for their inspiration, articles and information: *The Funeral Director*, *The Funeral Journal*, *Pharos*, *Thanos*, FIAT/IFTA, *The American Funeral Director Journal*, *Funerals of the Famous*, *The Funeral Times*, *The Immortalist* and so many others.

The National Association of Funeral Directors, Society of Allied Independent Funeral Directors, British Institute of Funeral Directors and British Institute of Embalmers.

Death: A User's Guide, by Tom Hickman (Delta, 2003), for some interesting points.

The Crown/Ministry of Defence.

Squadron Leader Rob Rowntree and his family for their help and support.

Scottish TV and Ginger TV.

Carole Bearden for her support and encouragement through the past sixteen years.

Newspapers, magazines and many journalists for their inspirational death tales.

The endless dedication of all those involved with the death-care industry.

Paul Darnell for his eagle eye and support.

My sons, Simon and Jonathan, my dad and Fred, my grandchildren – born and unborn – and all my family; God bless you all.

My friends Peter Hindley and Andrew Davis: thank you.

My friend Gino: *Ciao Ciao Bambino*.

Joanna and Jackie for hours of dedication.

All the staff at Albin's.

My mates Paul, Tom, Rick, Norman, Terry and Steve – the Wednesday Society.

The wonderful people of Bermondsey, Rotherhithe and South London.

And everybody mentioned in these books, even if by alias.

Barry George Dyer
Be lucky!

THE CAT AND THE CATAFALQUE

Now, at our local crematorium they have an interesting array of pets (if you can call them pets). There is the dove that was released at a previous funeral and didn't fly home, nesting instead in the trees and on top of the crematorium – it will fly down and eat seed almost out of your hand if you want it to. Then there are the tame squirrels that come up the steps and feed on peanuts that the staff bring in for them; they eat some and take some and bury them for another day. In turn, they are watched by crows, who then, as the squirrels leave, fly down to dig up the nuts and take them away to eat.

All in all, the wildlife up at the crematorium is fairly tame and very interesting to observe, but perhaps the most interesting animal at the crematorium is a wild tabby cat. I say wild, but that's just its origin, as in truth it is very tame. It has made its home downstairs where it is quite warm, not far from the furnaces, to be fed by the staff and live rather a charmed life. We occasionally see the cat around the grounds of the crematorium, or if it is a little cold it will sit near the car radiator for ten minutes to warm up. A very friendly animal.

At a recent funeral at the crematorium, the expression that cats have nine lives certainly proved true. We had arrived in good time for the service, which was to be taken by our local minister, Bill, a very kind gentleman. He greeted the family on the stairs of the crematorium, we played a little comforting music, and the family was seated. Next, the coffin was carried into the crematorium and placed on the catafalque.

We had actually started the service a few minutes late because one or two people had not turned up, but about five minutes into the service they arrived. We quietly opened the door for them so that they could slip in unnoticed at the rear of the chapel, but as the last person entered, the tabby cat ran up the stairs, through the legs of the conductor and into the crematorium service chapel, sitting itself down at the back.

We thought it best at this point not to make too much fuss; after all, the minister had seen the cat enter and was taking no notice, so better just to leave it quietly at the back. If we tried to catch the cat, it might run and cause a bit of a scene, unsettling the congregation. So the service continued for another ten minutes until we came to the point of committal. The cat had not moved, and our minister Bill read the words of committal and pushed the button that sets the catafalque in motion to close downwards.

Now, you have to remember that the catafalque is huge, bronze and extremely heavy. As it began to go down into the ground from about six and a half feet in the air, the cat strolled slowly forward, putting its head completely into the opening and watching the coffin go further and further downwards. Of course, what the cat had not noticed was that above it, closing down upon it and now only about a foot from its head, was the huge bronze lid that covers the opening in the ground at the top of the catafalque. The cat was only minutes from death.

The minister continued the committal – 'ashes to ashes, dust to dust, we commend the soul of our sister here departed' – and on the word 'commend', with the top of the catafalque only about six inches from the cat's head, brought his right foot across his left, pushing the cat into the opening just seconds before the catafalque closed. In his earlier days, Bill must have been some sort of footballer because it was a clean, beautifully timed precision strike, all carried out without any change of expression or alteration of his prescribed service.

At this point, there was a gasp from the mourners. Some thought that the minister had pushed the cat to its death, believing incorrectly that the coffin goes directly into the furnace. Others – including, may I say, the main mourners – thought the incident was hysterical, and some were of course just pleased to see that the cat had not been killed by the lid of the catafalque. Meanwhile, the cat was safe and well downstairs. It walked along to its little bed and blanket and went to sleep, completely unharmed or undisturbed by the incident.

Moments later, the service was over. As the family left the crematorium, shaking the minister's hand, they remarked that, although Mum hadn't much liked cats, she wouldn't have wanted it to be harmed in any way or come to a 'catastrophic' end. There was laughter all round, and I can assure you the family will never forget the day that the cat joined Mum on her final journey.

Needless to say, the cat has now been banned from the chapel area, but maybe it just brought a moment of light relief among a great deal of pain – not a bad thing, you might say. After all, I always maintain that laughter and tears are very much the same emotion.

INTRODUCTION

It was just past six o'clock on a dark Monday morning, perhaps the first cold morning of November 2004. I was sitting quietly in the office listening to talkSPORT on the radio and reflecting on the week to come. Bill (another Bill – not the cat's rescuer) had just popped across the road to get my morning paper, something he does daily. Jackie and Maureen were chatting in the kitchen, and pretty soon the staff of Albin's would begin to arrive. Jon Fletcher would probably pull in first – he likes to miss the traffic coming from just past the Bluewater shopping centre – followed by Simon, Jon, Greg and Paul if they were lucky with the traffic. One by one, the staff that mean so much to Albin's would begin to arrive.

The leaves were falling quite violently from the trees today. Two of our people were in Iraq, bringing back a soldier from the Black Watch who sadly had lost his life the previous week. As I looked slowly through the funerals I had been asked to conduct that week, I noted so many names that had been familiar to me over the years. I was truly sad to see them on this list, and yet again I was reminded of the importance of every moment that life gives us, and realised that, for me, there was still more to say about the struggle of life and death.

The book you are about to read (I hope!) – *Strong Shoulders* – is the last of the books I shall write (well, that's the plan at the moment, anyway). As I look at the painting in our reception that reflects the history of the past, the present and the future – my dad, Fred, myself in the middle, my sons Simon and Jonathan – it occurs to me that the rule *Don't Drop the Coffin*, the title of my first book, is still very safe in the hands of all these people (and family) I work with. Just like me, they'd say *Bury My Heart in Bermondsey* – that's the second book in the trilogy – and this new title of *Strong Shoulders* is clearly reflected in all of us. Despite this being a trilogy, this is actually my fourth book as I wrote *Final Departures* along the way, a book I had wanted to write for years, looking at funeral practices all around the world.

So why *Strong Shoulders*? Well, believe me, to carry a coffin daily you need strong shoulders. A funeral director also needs strong shoulders for people to cry on, shoulders that have to be very strong and broad because bereavement brings so much anger and grief that is often directed his way. So you see, it is not just the ever-necessary physical strength that a funeral director needs, but also the strength of compassion, a firm yet kind heart and, believe it or not, a warm and welcoming smile. If 'Don't drop the coffin, son' were the first words my dad said to me, next certainly came 'You need strong shoulders, boy.' It was not until many years later that I realised the true meaning of 'strong shoulders'.

Writing books and appearing on TV have certainly brought some recognition. A few Sundays ago, as I got out of my car at my house in Rotherhithe on the riverfront, I turned to notice a pleasureboat only a few feet away from the edge of the river wall that goes along the front of my house. As these boats sail down the river, they give a guided tour with the history of all the wonderful places the river rolls past. Imagine my amazement as I turned to hear '. . . and on your right, just getting out of his car, is Barry Albin-Dyer from the TV series *Don't Drop the Coffin*, and that's his house . . .' – and people were waving. I just stood in amazement. I reflected after that it must have been one of the riverboat lightermen who eat in the café I go in on Saturday mornings with the boys. You've got to laugh, haven't you? – I'm now an item on the riverboat tour. In Bermondsey, that's real fame!

Having now written four books – and got used to being recognised sometimes – I have promised myself that this will be the last. I want it to say so much that I feel is still left unsaid. Such is my story – not my personal autobiography but the story of my life, my work, the role that life and death play in our lives and, never to be forgotten, the awful power of bereavement. I hope that if you get to read *Final Departures*, it will take you a little out of yourself and leave you somewhat amazed by the incredible cultures and strange things that people do concerning death around the world. If you have read *Don't Drop the Coffin* and *Bury My Heart in Bermondsey*, you will by now know me a little better, and I hope that the stories leave you with contentment and comfort, but most of all a smile relieving the fear. I can only hope that you enjoy *Strong Shoulders* in the same way. I hope that my new readers (both of you!) won't find me too boring.

Thank you.
Barry Dyer

ON THE STREET WHERE I LIVED

Being born in Bermondsey, South London, has always given me a great sense of pride, especially being born in Guy's Hospital, which I regard as a great stroke of luck and indeed even a privilege and an honour. Guy's Hospital and the Evelina Children's Hospital were to play a very helpful part in my early childhood as I suffered with whooping cough, leaving me with a shadow across my lung. This meant that Guy's Hospital became a regular visiting place as the staff helped to restore my health.

Whenever any childhood illnesses needed specialist handling, off you were sent to the Evelina, and to have both of these wonderful institutions on your doorstep was indeed good luck. As a child, you were sent to one of them for everything: inoculations, dentistry, having your tonsils out and more delicate operations (ouch, I'll say no more). You name it, Guy's and the Evelina provided it. Mind you, I will never forget the terrible smell of gas when having early teeth removed – so sickly I can't even bear to think about it. Thank God we don't have to have that any more. Later on in life, too, the hospital was of great help after I had a dreadful altercation with a post office van from which I definitely came off worse. So here is a personal thanks to you, Guy's and the Evelina – not that I liked visiting you at the time. Then, I was always quite scared of those two hospitals and the short walk Mum and I had to get there. Naturally, I now realise it was for my own good, so I'm very grateful.

Guy's was and still is a wonderful teaching hospital, and who would have thought that this little boy born in Bermondsey – Barry George Dyer – would be one of the senior members of the fundraising committee for the new Evelina Children's Hospital? This gives me a huge link with the past and overwhelms me with pride and tradition. Me, a little Bermondsey boy, helping to raise up to £10 million to help equip the new hospital. My mum would approve if she were with us now – not that she has ever really left me, as I have often explained. When she died I was seventeen years old. Sadly, Guy's was unable to do anything for her, which gave me a rude awakening to the realities of this life. I couldn't imagine that Guy's wouldn't get Mum well again. I couldn't really accept, even at the age of seventeen and having grown up around the funeral business, that she would not get well. Isn't that what we all do – refuse to accept the inevitable?

You see, I had had such a happy childhood, even, believe

it or not, living over a funeral director's. There were restrictions, of course. I couldn't play my radiogram, as they were called in those days, when I wanted – only very first thing in the morning before the office got underway downstairs. I couldn't have other kids in to play or have sleepovers: who would want to sleep over at the funeral director's? Not many of my friends, I can promise you. But although my memories encompass so much of Bermondsey, I guess that my days living above the shop were, in a way, a golden era for me, even if at times a little lonely.

It was a little old Dickensian shop without a bathroom or hot water other than our little Ascot geyser, as they were known in those days, which provided just enough hot water for the sink. My mum, a very clean lady, would regularly make me scrub down, and Friday was tin-bath night in the kitchen in front of the fire. My bedroom was at the very top of the house. Although it was a little bit damp and certainly cold, it was a large bedroom with lots of cupboard space. Some of the cupboards were so big you could hide in them, and I kept my comics stacked in them as well. Number 62 Jamaica Road, Bermondsey SE16 – that was the address of the old shop called F. A. Albin & Sons Funeral Directors (undertakers). The light from the street lamp shone directly through my window, illuminating my room at night.

I loved Jamaica Road, the street where I lived. It was so busy and full of life and wonderful characters. Although some would have said that I was living at the dead end of life, it was quite the opposite. Everybody knew Fred Albin and my dad, my mum, old Mr Albin; they were pillars of society. Likewise, everyone knew who I was from a very young age, which could, of course, be quite a disadvantage for a young boy. I mean, if anything went wrong or if I got up to any mischief, like normal kids do, I was immediately caught and reported to my dad without delay, and he naturally took the appropriate action. On the other hand, there were advantages too. The man who owned the fish shop knew my dad so well that I would always get an extra portion of crackling on my fish and chips, and I'd get an extra doughnut at Edwards' the bakers. Every once in a while, I would see one of our cars on its way back to the garage, and I would get a lift home. That was great, as I loved the old cars. The pride of our fleet today is still the lovely old Rolls-Royce hearse, still working regularly and rolling around the streets of Bermondsey as proud as ever. Some things need never change if you take enough care to preserve them.

But what of Jamaica Road and the people who lived in it? Right next door to Albin's shop was a tiny little park, only about fifty yards by fifty yards, which bordered on the back of our workshop fence. That became the centre of my early great sporting career. It was Wembley Stadium for me and some of the local kids who used to play in it. There, I scored wonderful world-class goals (as I seem to remember, anyway) against some of the best goalkeepers in the world. I also became the Freddie Trueman of Bermondsey, regularly sending the stumps flying into the air. And here my golfing career started (and ended, really) as we also used it as a little putting green. Rain or shine, any time of day, the park was open for us because the fence was only five feet high and easy to jump over even if the Parky had closed it at five o'clock in the evening. How I loved those days. Looking back, I had really not a worry in the world – and that's how your life should be as a child.

Just the other side of our shop in Jamaica Road was Jack's, the pet shop. He kept mice, hamsters, budgerigars, canaries, rabbits, kittens, fishing bait and corn feed. Jack had a son called John, whom I occasionally still see; he was in a group called The Wildcats, and I always wanted to be able to play the guitar like him. He never played sport with us in the park, dedicating himself instead to fishing and playing the guitar in his group. Next door to Jack's was Alice's, the sweet shop, where you could buy broken crisps, broken *Smith's* crisps if you don't mind, in tiny packets for a penny a packet, and five-for-a-penny gobstoppers. Inside was an array of drinks and old-fashioned jars of sweets. Alice was quite a strict lady – you behaved yourself when you went into her shop.

Alongside her was Albuy's, the wool shop, where Mum and Nan used to get their knitting wool. Then Holgrave's the florist and Stannit's the café. Then the Rising Sun pub, Hodges' the fish shop and another little confectionery and cigarette shop, the name of which escapes me. Next came the chemist, with everything you needed for coughs and colds. Sid Frankall was the pharmacist, and our Joan often worked there. Then there was Harvey and Thompson, the pawnbrokers and jewellers. A few houses and then St James' Church.

Directly opposite the shop was Sweetland's the butchers, a little bakery, and then Armer's the bean factory, and the little oil shop on the corner. Just behind it was the youth club of the Cambridge University Mission (or Come You Mugs, as we knew it), where I spent many happy hours as a lad with Snowy Davoll, one of the leaders. Then I remember a little shoe shop and boot-mender's called Ballard's (so Connie Downes reminds me). Next was a lovely little shop that used to sell records and stay open until about 6.30 on a Saturday evening. I would sit indoors and watch *Juke Box Jury*, and if a new song that I liked came up, I would run straight over to the shop to try to order it for the following Saturday. Next in line was the Co-op foodstore and, believe it or not, the Co-operative Funeral Directors. They never did very well in Bermondsey in those days and closed in the early 1970s. Bermondsey people were loyal and loved Albin's, and I love their loyalty, as it is – with their kindness and hospitality – their greatest asset.

Alongside the Co-op was the Lilliput Hall pub, the place to be seen in those days. Opposite that was, as it still is today, the Barracks and Army Cadets' Hall, and tracing back along that side of the road was Robinson's the electrical shop and, on the corner, a lovely old fruit and veg shop. To the side of that sat a little cigarette, sweet and ice cream shop where I would often go for my dad on an errand.

Along the road a little further and there was Robinson's the bike shop – he was the son of Robinson's the electrical shop who went into business for himself, and very successfully too. Then there were a few houses as you came along back to the park I played in and back to Albin's.

Everybody knew everybody then. As I often say, 'we were all one'. Tramlines were still set in the road, never having been moved from years back. In those days, the road used to have stalls in it and be a real hive of activity. As I was growing up, those disappeared; the tramlines were still there, but the bus route was a 47 or a 188. The 47 took you in one direction to London Bridge and in the other to the Elephant and Castle. The 188, I seem to remember, went to Farnborough or Lewisham. In the late 1960s, just across the way from Jamaica Road and under Spenlow House was a little café called The Tasty Freeze. I remember the opening day, when everything was half price and I had this amazing item called a Dusseldorf, which was like a huge hot dog, and a milkshake. They even had pop music playing and imported *Mad* magazine from America. Fantastic. I had never seen anything like it. Definitely the place to go.

What days they were! As a young man living over a funeral director's it seemed OK to me. After all, I didn't know any different. So I have come to the conclusion that it is only what we know that changes things – the way we can't miss what we didn't have. As the years pass by, memories become fonder. Even the one when I was just like Oliver Twist, sitting in the cellar with a candle with all the coffins surrounding me, waiting for the opportunity to pass the coffins up into the main workshop through the office. It has less of a shiver and more of a warmth about it now, and we should never forget that happiness is found throughout the journey and not just at the end.

I still live only about a mile from that actual spot, and whenever I pass through Jamaica Road, which is now known as Old Jamaica Road, a floodgate opens and passionate memories flow through my veins and fill my mind with happiness and nostalgia.

CHILDHOOD THINGS

Whenever we look back, the memories often seem clearer, usually happier and often comforting – the 'Good Old Days', we call them. Surely, then, today will eventually become the Good Old Days to our children. Or is it in truth all a myth? Are we really looking back and being comforted by simple memories and senses, smells, taste, touch, sounds, photographs, visions, all of them in themselves from the past? With all these thoughts in mind, I have decided to write down, not in any particular order of time or preference, under headings, some of the things that I personally love to recall, so why not join me for a few minutes if your memory brushes the same years? Even if only one thing in this list relates to you, maybe the nostalgia will take you on a similar trip to mine here, travelling over many decades. So here we go.

Sweets (in jars, bars, bags and boxes)

Sherbet lemons
Pear drops
Barley sugar
Winter mixtures
Cough candy
Merry maids
Lucky numbers
Bull's eyes
Gobstoppers
Hundreds and thousands
Liquorice
Coconut mushrooms
Chews
Chocolate raisins
Chocolate nuts
Fox's glacier mints
Murray mints
Wrigley's spearmint
Bubble gum
Jelly babies
Black jacks
Fruit salads
Rhubarb and custard
Humbugs
Jelly beans
Wine gums

CHILDHOOD THINGS

Fruit drops
Marshmallows
Desiccated coconut
American hard gums
Nut crunch
Nut rock
Honeycomb
Sweet shrimps
Sweet bananas
Gummy bears
Sugar baby dummys
Aniseed balls
Toffees – hard and soft
Poppets
Maltesers
Roses
Munchies
Black Magic
Cadbury's Dairy Milk
Milk Tray
Dairy Box
Bournville
Toffetts
Milky Bars
Nestlé bars
Fruit and nut
Aero
Kit-Kat

Mars bars
Milky Way
Bounty bars
Raspberry Ruffle bars
Galaxy
Cadbury's Flake
Crunchies
Turkish delight
Jamboree bags (full of goodies)
Sherbet dabs
Liquorice pipes
Liquorice shoelaces

I am sure I have missed a lot, but can't you just taste all those lovely sweets?

Ice creams (and lollies, of course)

Raspberry ripple
Vanilla
Neapolitan
Strawberry
Chocolate
Mint choc chip
Lemon sorbet
Lemon ice
Mister Whippy
Orange Maid lollies

CHILDHOOD THINGS

Zooms
Mivvys
Twisters
Jubblys (lovely jubbly)
Choc ices

Cool and refreshing, all of them.

Soft drinks (my favourites, anyway)

Dandelion and burdock (bought down the East Lane)
Cherryade
Limeade
Raspberryade
Lemonade (in fact any kind of 'ade' you can think of)
Cream soda
Ginger ale
Lucozade
Coca-Cola
Pepsi Cola
Ribena
Lemon and barley
Milkshakes – chocolate, banana, vanilla, strawberry,
    raspberry, lime, orange, pineapple (you name it, they can
    shake it)

Foods (my favourites, anyway)

Rock and chips
Skate and chips
Cod and chips
Saveloy and pease pudding
Pie and mash
Jellied eels (not to my liking, but my old nan loved them)
Percy Dalton peanuts
Hot dogs
Wimpys
Doozle dogs (huge hot dogs with ketchup)
Telfer's meat pies
Doughnuts
Doughnut rings
Biscuits – coconut fingers, custard creams, shortcake, chocolate, Nice, Rich Tea, digestives, arrowroot
Stews with dumplings
Roast beef and Yorkshire pudding
Sausage and mash
Full English breakfast
Coco Pops
Cornflakes
Frosties
Rice Krispies
Shredded Wheat
Weetabix
Porridge (winter only!)

Rhubarb and custard
Jelly and ice cream
Fruit salad
Baked beans on toast
Spaghetti on toast
Liver and bacon

You could go on and on.

And from years gone by . . .

Comics (the ones I used to get, anyway)
Victor
Valiant
Beano
Dandy
Hotspur
New Musical Express

Toys (still fresh in my memory)
A yellow and red fireman that walked up a ladder
A helicopter that spun round on an axle
Hercules bikes
A Tri-ang clockwork engine
Tri-ang scooters
My favourite musical teddy (still alive and well today)
A Hornby train set
Charlie Chugg Chugg (a battery-operated engine) – me and
    my dad's favourite

A steam tractor
Meccano
Scooby Doos
Hula hoops
Monopoly
Cluedo
Spy Ring
Rubik's Cube
Snakes and ladders
Ludo
Chess
Draughts
Dominos
Plasticine
Blow football
Subbuteo
Cowboy outfit
Scalextric
Yo-yos
Parker pens
Ball-bearing scooters
Carts made of old pram wheels
My magic set (I really wanted to be a magician when I was
    a kid)
Potato men
Painting by numbers
Soldiers
A lovely fort (which my dad had made for me)

A pedal car
All my lovely sports gear
Cricket set
Table tennis set
Billiard set
Football and my fantastic football boots (Bobby Charlton specials)
Old Stanley Matthews boots with leather studs
Mitres, Golas, Adidas, Brazilianos (all in black, of course – very tasteful)
The Old Den (the Millwall football ground in Coldblow Lane)
Rattles
Rosettes
Scarves
Bobble hats
Arsenal vs Wolves (the only football game I went to with my dad – a golden memory)
Endless books and, of course, a full set of encyclopaedias

I was certainly well endowed with toys, and these are just a few I remember clearly.

TV programmes
There are far too many of these to mention, but the following come to mind:

Watch with Mother

Picture Book
Rag, Tag and Bobtail
The Woodentops
Bill and Ben
Andy Pandy (not forgetting Looby Loo and Teddy, of
    course)
Dr Who
Treasure Island
The Adventures of Twizzle
Four Feather Falls
Torchy the Battery Boy
Fireball XL5 (I think that is what it was called)
Match of the Day (still on BBC2 in those days)
Sarah and Hoppity
Captain Pugwash
Star Trek
Sunday Night at the London Palladium
Dangerman
The Saint
The Prisoner
Maverick
Wells Fargo
Bonanza
Laramie
Wagon Train
Rawhide
Have Gun, Will Travel
Rin Tin Tin

CHILDHOOD THINGS

Zoo Time
Popeye
The Flintstones
Huckleberry Hound
Yogi Bear
Pixie and Dixie (and Jinksy the Cat)
Adam Adamant (not to be confused with the pop star Adam
   Ant!)
Criss Cross Quiz
Dotto
What's My Line?
The Morecambe and Wise Show
Juke Box Jury
Top of the Pops
Ready, Steady, Go!
Four Just Men
Whiplash
Perry Mason
Branded
The Banana Splits
The Dick Van Dyke Show
I Love Lucy
The Beverley Hillbillies
My Favourite Martian
Steptoe and Son
Bootsy and Snudge
The Army Game
Crossroads

Coronation Street
The Harry Worth Show

Radio
The Clithero Kid
Sing Something Simple (how depressing)
The Sunday night chart show (the top forty records of the
    time)
Family Favourites (on a Sunday morning)
The Man in Black (terrifying in those days)
The Guy Mitchell Singers
Desert Island Discs

More TV
I never listened to much radio in those days, so back to TV
for a moment.

The Black and White Minstrel Show
The Golden Shot
The Invisible Man (Pete Brady)
The Flying Nun
The Andy Williams Show
The Twilight Zone
Lost in Space
Emergency – Ward 10
Charlie Chan
Fabian of the Yard (I am sure that was what it was called)
Dixon of Dock Green

28

The Liver Birds
Z Cars
Man about the House
Doctor in the House
Quatermass and the Pit
The Ghost Squad
The Avengers
The Lone Ranger
Zorro
That Was the Week That Was
Monty Python's Flying Circus
The 1948 Show
Gideon's Way
Noddy
On the Buses
Lassie
The Three Stooges
Mr Ed
My Three Sons
The Monkees
Mork and Mindy
Double Your Money
Take Your Pick
The Charlie Drake Show (I think he originated from Bermondsey)
The Max Bygraves Show (another Bermondsey Boy)
Tommy Steele specials ('Little White Bull', etc.)
Casey Jones (a kind of Western – he was the train driver)

Don't Drop the Coffin (who said that?)
Route 66
Car 54 Where Are You? (two of my favourites, these last two)

I'd better end there because my memories of TV are strong, and I could go on for ever. I must confess, I'm still a fan of TV now.

And just to finish, in no particular order, a few things that come to my mind indiscriminately. Simple memories that are no more.

The first two records I bought on the same day: *Wonderful Land* by The Shadows, and *Transister Sister* by Robbie Storm
Record tokens – do you remember those?
45s, 78s and 33⅓s (all record sizes, those)
Elvis
The Beatles
The Kinks
The Rolling Stones
The Hollies
The Tremeloes
Peter and Gordon
Simon and Garfunkel
The Settlers

David Bowie
The Dave Clark Five
The Animals
Freddie and the Dreamers
The Searchers
Slade
The Righteous Brothers
Billy Fury

Tank tops
Vests
Idiot mittens (thanks again for those, Mum)
Scholl sandals
Doc Marten's boots
Platform shoes
Cuban heel boots
Adidas Three Stripe
Drainpipes
Flares
Ben Sherman shirts
Fred Perry's
Mohair suits
Dog's-tooth-check trousers
Snake belts
Hot pants
Topless dresses (yes, topless)
Mini skirts
Midi skirts

Pantaloons
Ski pants
Stilettos (not that I wore any of the last few, of course, but
    I certainly enjoyed them being worn by the fairer sex)
Brut aftershave
Old Spice aftershave
Imperial Leather aftershave
Hai Karate aftershave
Kipper ties
Paisley shirts
Button-down collars
Pinned collars
Bomber jackets
Duffel coats
Anoraks
St Christopher charms
Charm bracelets
'Ticka-ticka-Timex' watches
Accurist watches ('acc your ankle, acc your knee')
Identity bracelets (very fashionable in the 1960s and 1970s)
Plimsolls
Full-length leather jackets
Three-quarter leathers
Suede coats
Signet rings
Birthstone rings
My Hank Marvin glasses (from The Shadows, of course)
Winkle-pickers

Chelsea boots
Donkey jackets
Parkas (Mods' coats)
Harrington jackets
Squire shoes

Go-faster stripes on my car (Starsky and Hutch stripes –
     well, there's a TV programme I forgot)
Ford Capri
1600E Cortina
Rover 90
VW (my lovely little red 1300)
My first car – a Ford Popular ('sit up and beg')
My second car, a Morris Traveller (it looked like a boat on
     wheels)
Bubble cars
Three-wheeler 'Del Boy' cars
Messerschmitts (the car built on the cockpit of a
     Messerschmitt, a little three-wheeler)

The muffin man
The toffee apple man
The coal man
The milkman
The newspaper man
The electric man
The gas man
The Radio Rentals man

STRONG SHOULDERS

The knife-sharpening man
The encyclopaedia salesman
The Hoover salesman
The bread delivery man
The Corona man (who used to deliver fizzy drinks to our
    street)

All straight to your door.

Crisps in any flavour you like, as long as it was plain, with a
bag of salt inside. At first, there were only Smith's Crisps,
but then they were closely followed by Golden Wonder.

Cigarette and tobacco brands such as:
Peter Stuyvesant
Old Holborn
Woodbine
Senior Service
Embassy
Benson and Hedges
Marlborough
Golden Virginia (pipe and cigarette tobaccos)
Strand ('You're never alone with a Strand' – or so the advert
    would say)

Record-players
Tape-recorders
Radiograms

CHILDHOOD THINGS

Transistor radios
'Press button A and B' telephone boxes
Police whistles
Old Grandad Popes (little horse and carriages that used to
    run around Bermondsey all those years ago)
My dad's mouth organ
My dad's accordion (he was quite musical, my dad)
Our first Rediffusion television
The old accumulator radios
Gas fires

Then there were the games we played as kids:
British bulldog
Hopscotch
Knock down ginger
Postman's knock
Five stones
Ally gobs
Hide and seek
Kiss chase
True love, dare, kiss or promise
Rounders

My memories go on and on.

Lambrettas
Mods and rockers
Teddy boys

Flock wallpaper
Holiday camps – Butlins, Pontins, etc.
Caravans
My old trombone (from the school band)
My old drum kit (well, one drum and a cymbal!)

Ahh, those memories and places will never fade from my mind. As you can see, I was a style fashion and food guru even then. If I have bored you for the last few minutes, please indulge me in what may be the last book I write. But if I have whetted your appetite for the past, that's a good job done. There is no harm in a nostalgic journey back in time now and again, as long as we don't live in the past. And don't be disillusioned by thinking that I liked all the things I have mentioned – some I completely disliked!
 Happy days.

The things people do

Eating fish and chips out of newspaper (it always tasted better).
    Pouring a hot cup of tea into the saucer to blow on it and cool it down, then drinking it from the saucer (my dad and Fred always did that in my mum's kitchen, but never, of course, while having tea with the vicar).
    Eating a Kit-Kat bar by nibbling the chocolate from the outside and then eating the biscuit last.
    Biting the bottom and the top corners off a Penguin bar

before putting one end into a hot cup of tea and the other into your mouth. Then you can suck the tea through the bar until it is saturated, push the whole bar into your mouth and eat it. (It sounds disgusting but it tastes wonderful – and it's today's kids who have taught me that one.)

Putting the tiny dog-ends of self-made cigarettes that can no longer be smoked into a tin to make yet another new one.

When drinking hot tea without milk (in my experience, Persian tea), putting a cube of sugar into your mouth and drinking the tea through the sugar to get the sweetness you require. (This is really quite proper behaviour in Iran, and it tastes delicious.)

Sucking the sherbet out of the ends of sherbet lemons and leaving the rest of the sweet.

Dipping biscuits in your tea – 'dunking', we call it (mmm, nothing better).

Egg soldiers (bits of toast cut into fingers to dip in your boiled eggs).

Eating a doughnut without licking your lips (impossible).

The more modern condition of constantly switching TV channels but never watching one single programme (guilty!).

Blowing bubbles from a bubble gum and making dreadful noises.

Drinking your favourite drink, whatever it may be, from the bottle rather than a glass.

Taking the cream from rich cream milk to put on your cereal (considered very unhealthy today).

Splitting open custard cream biscuits and licking out the custard cream.

Eating bread and butter and leaving your crusts.

The amount of sauce that people put on the side of their dinner plates to eat – horseradish, mint, ketchup, mustard, etc. – in truth, never to be eaten but instead left on the side of the plate. (Perhaps on the West Norwood Cemetery mausoleum of the Colmans – the famous mustard-making family – it should say, 'We made our money from what you left on the plate.')

Brown boots worn at a funeral. (I ask you, brown boots when everyone else is wearing black! Well I never!)

Picking up the horse poo after a funeral and people wanting to keep it as manure for their gardens (a good old tradition, that one – it's supposed to bring good luck).

And there are quite a few disgusting practices definitely not to be investigated in this book!

1

DEATH IS NOTHING AT ALL

Death is nothing at all
I have only slipped away into the next room.
I am I. You are you.
Whatever we were to each other, that we still are.
Call me by my old familiar name,
Speak to me in the easy way which you always used.
Put no difference into your tone,
wear no air of solemnity or sorrow.
Laugh as we always laughed at the little jokes we enjoyed
    together.
Play, smile, think of me, pray for me.

Let my name be the household word that it always was.
Let it be spoken without effect, without the ghost of a
    shadow in it.
Life means all that it ever meant. It is the same as it ever
    was.

There is absolutely unbroken continuity.
What is death but a negligible accident?
Why should I be out of mind because I am out of sight?
I am but waiting for you, for an interval,
somewhere very near, just around the corner.
All is well.
Nothing is past, nothing is lost.
One brief moment, and all will be as it was before.

(Canon Henry Scott Holland)

They say that nothing can get in the way of progress or an Albin's funeral, and that's certainly true in Bermondsey. In truth, of course, everybody is afraid of dying, and perhaps those who say they are not have a different kind of fear. Maybe people are not afraid of death itself but of the make-over at the undertaker's. We do try to make the deceased look lifelike, as lifelike as possible anyway, which some people might say defeats the purpose. After all, it is quite hard to feel bad for somebody who looks better than you do, and, funny as it sounds, that is often the case. When we enter a chapel, are we in truth afraid to see somebody whom we have known or whom we love because looking at them means we are looking at our own certain future, death being the ultimate journey that we all eventually make?

When we are afraid, we sometimes turn to lighter words and survive using humour, like an old Bermondsey friend of mine who died leaving me a specific request relating to the last song to be played as we left the crematorium. Just to have the last laugh, he requested 'Fall In and Follow Me', and with the strength, passion and humour for which Bermondsey is famous, everyone sang along with that final tune, acknowledging the lighter side of Brian's last request. In a note that Brian left me, telling me exactly how the funeral should be conducted, he went on to say, 'Barry, you know me pretty well and I have been to plenty of your funerals – you could say that I am a professional mourner – and I have to say that I am much more comfortable with funerals, certainly much more than I am with weddings. After all, at a funeral the worst thing that can happen has already happened. A wedding, however, might have a lot more up its sleeve, so do me proud, mate, wontcha?' I remember clearly that as Brian left the shop on the last time I ever saw him, he looked round and said, 'Bal, remember, mate, no matter what anyone tells you, you are the greatest boxer in Bermondsey. All right, ta-ta, be lucky.' I will be, Brian – thanks for the memories.

Another loyal old customer of mine, Danny, still alive and well, thank God, phoned me one morning: 'Bal, can you help me, mate? I know you often speak at funerals and it's beautiful, but I've been asked to do the same at my cousin's. Can you give me a helping hand? They want me to do the urology and I don't know what to do.'

Urology, I thought – has he got a kidney problem?

'Dan, of course I'll help you, mate, but I think you mean the eulogy, don't you?'

'Well, urology, eulogy, it's all the same thing.'

'No, not quite, Dan.'

'Well, I'll be taking the piss either way, you know what I mean, mate? Can you help me?'

'Of course, Dan,' I replied, still laughing from his comment. 'Pop down tomorrow morning at about eight o'clock and we'll go through it together,' which of course we did.

Danny phoned me several days later having completed the 'urology' at his cousin's funeral up in Sheffield and told me it was beautiful. 'Bal, it went lovely. We laughed and cried – perfect, mate.' Urology – great one, Danny.

You see, I tell you again and again in my books that my job is not a miserable one. People are as lovely as they can be, and even when they are not they are still lovely because bereavement, however near or far, can make you say the strangest of things – we have all got to make allowances for that. These things are often said in nervousness or a state of numbness. Sometimes they tell the truth too clearly and that can be extremely painful for all concerned. The funeral director often has to just take it on the chin, whether it is said in anger or is just very sad or, of course, funny.

One family I had arranged a funeral for were all together in the front room when I popped round with the death certificate that I had collected from the Registrar for them. There was Tom, the dad, who had lost his wife Emily (Em as she was known in Bermondsey). The couple's three daughters and four sons were all in the front room with Dad.

We were due to bring her home to rest in that very same front room the next day. As I passed the certificate over, explaining the cause of death, which was heart failure, the old man said, as clear as day and I'll never forget, 'Oh girls, thank God she didn't die of anything serious.'

There was complete silence in the room until one of the boys piped up with, 'Well, that's bloody serious enough, Dad – Mum's dead, it can't get any worse.'

'Gawd help us,' he said, 'I don't know what I'm saying. I was just thinking, you know, I was worried that she had some terrible illness like cancer and we didn't know that she was in pain.'

'That's all right, Dad; don't worry, we know,' and with a little laughter and a few tears they all got through a very difficult moment by holding on to each other.

There is nothing wrong with having an opinion about things. It's a well-known fact in Bermondsey that if you put two Bermondsey people in a room, you will certainly get three opinions, but again there's no harm in that. After all, the older we get, the better we are in all walks of life.

Following that line of thought and looking back, I'm sure I was a wonderful footballer – that's what my memory tells me, anyway. But the truth of many events, of course, is hidden far deeper inside us, and in the overwhelming experience of bereavement that truth comes to the surface and can be terribly difficult to deal with. Again, in the fear of that moment we often turn to laughter to suppress our feelings or, more honestly, hide them. Like the dear old –

but saucy – lady who sat in our reception having lost her husband of forty-five years and said, 'We always used to joke, you know. He used to say, "You go first, Lil, cos I like being on top," but I used to say to him, "It don't matter, Bill, being underneath is just as much fun." Well, that's how it will have to be now. He might have liked being on top in life, but in death he's going to have to remain underneath, the way God planned it.' You see, Lil was just trying to see the bright side – if there was such a thing – of her loss.

There are, of course, the more immature forms of laughter in our business. Take, for example, the kids who would run into the shop and shout out, 'Mr Albin, got any empty boxes?' and run out again, or shout over the fence, 'Oy, mister, it ain't the cough you're coughing, it's the coffin they carry yer off in' – the silly little rhymes that children used to make up that you don't hear any more. 'Albin's boxes are the best, they fit you tight across the chest' or 'Mr Albin, do you have a skeleton staff on at the weekends?' All very childish, of course, but still reflecting the natural fear of death that even kids have.

Then there are the funny but innocent things that children say in all honesty without knowing. One little girl, about four or five years old, sat on her grandad's knee and said, 'Grandad, when you die do you become a frog?'

Grandad was obviously quite shocked by this question and replied, 'No, why do you ask?'

'Well,' said the granddaughter, 'Mummy says when you

croak, we're all going to go to Disneyland. I can't wait to go to Disneyland.'

The grandad, laughing at the child's innocence, simply said, 'We'd better go all together before I really croak it,' which left his granddaughter jumping for joy. So from that simple enquiry some good has come, as well as the clear philosophy to live each day while you can and take every opportunity while you still have the chance. It's clearly too late when you are gone.

Only the other week, I was conducting a horsedrawn funeral at the Precious Blood Church, which lies just off Southwark Street at the Borough underneath the railway arches. Now very few things spook horses – not our Fred and George, anyway – but one thing they particularly do not like is railway arches, especially when a train rumbles over the tracks and the noise startles them. Once we had the family settled in church, the coffin having already been taken in the night before as is quite common with Catholic funerals, I came out and groomed for the horseman, standing in front of the horses. I thought it might just steady them if a train crossed overhead.

While I was standing there and idly passing the time with the horseman, George (the horse we named after my dad) lifted his head high. I commented to him, 'There's a big proud George, good boy.' At that moment, a train rumbled across the arch. Fred, a little startled, also lifted his head a little, which naturally spooked George. George's reaction was to sneeze violently, covering me from head to toe in, for want of a more polite term, horse snot. My glasses were speckled, my lovely striped funeral suit, even my shoes were full of it. Fred made a high-pitched whinny, as if laughing at me. The boys laughed too, not believing their luck in witnessing such an event happening to their boss. With the help of one of the lads, I retreated to the rear car where we had some water and cloths for car-cleaning that were quickly converted to snot-cleaning materials. Not the most pleasant experience, I can promise you! You never know what is going to happen next when you are conducting a funeral. The golden rule must always be 'preparation, preparation, preparation', and the second golden rule, yes, again 'preparation, preparation, and preparation'.

We have all heard the old actors' cry that you should never work with children or animals, but as funeral directors we of course have to work with both at times. Fortunately, the only animals we have to work with are horses and occasionally doves, albeit both very messy animals at times. You have just seen how unpredictable horses can be, but doves I always find to be very reliable. Nowadays, doves are often released by hand at gravesides or in the garden of remembrance outside the crematorium at the end of the funeral, symbolising the freeing of the spirit or soul from the body. We have our own dove man, Warren, who looks after the doves beautifully and cares greatly for them. It is inevitable, though, that as you take doves out of their cage, 99 per cent of the time they will produce some mess in your hand, something you try to be discreet about and cover up. 'Grin and bear it' is the policy here, but that can be very difficult if it is a little runny and seeps through your fingers to drop on the toes of your brogue shoes – as happened recently! People always see the funny side of it, and, as ever, we find that a little laugh lightens the day.

But why do people always laugh at bodily functions? We are strange beings, aren't we? After all, no horsedrawn funeral is complete without one of the horses urinating, passing wind or producing some manure – very useful for the garden, I suppose. But it does make the noble horse, or the beautiful white dove soaring into the sky, a little less lovely.

My son Jonathan was conducting a funeral one very hot day in June. It was a large funeral, and each of eight brothers and sisters had asked for a dove to release. This meant, of course, that by the time Jonathan had removed the eighth dove from the basket, the man holding the first one had been doing so for quite some time. Unfortunately, doves have their lungs in quite a prominent position, and if you hold them too tightly you can prevent them breathing properly. It is therefore imperative that you hold them gently and with great care. As the prayer was being said and Jonathan was asking for the doves to be released, he noticed that the head of the first dove was dropping. As the other seven flew off, the man holding it said, 'I think this one's had it, Jon; shall we put it down with Mum? She wouldn't mind and we bought the grave for two anyway.'

'No, no, don't do that, Jim,' said Jonathan. 'The dove's

just a little overcome. It's fainted but it's OK, it's not dead.'

Jonathan gently took the dove, opened its wings a little and breathed on it for a moment. A few minutes later, the dove came round and was able to fly off and join its pals. Young Jim would have had the poor little dove dead and buried in minutes. Perhaps he felt a little comfort that his mum would not have been on her own in the grave, but the dove survived to fly another day.

While we are on the subject of animals, there is, in our main yard, inside a glass cover, a beautiful horsedrawn hearse from 1864, fully renovated and in wonderful condition. It is well worth a visit if you are interested in old horsedrawn carriages, and it really is a picture. In the evening, it has lamps and a floodlit interior. To make it even more authentic, I have the horse blanket, the reins and the whip all on view. I take pride in looking round it every few days to make sure it is clean and looks well. One day, I noticed that a piece of horse rein was missing – extremely strange – so I asked the lads whether they knew anything about it. But nobody did. A few days later, the piece that goes around the horse's head and carries the plumes had disappeared. I began to wonder whether somebody was getting in at night and taking these things.

A few days later, getting into my car one evening, I spied a town fox that had slunk in through the railings from the park. He was up on the horsedrawn carriage and was pulling on another rein, which he eventually loosened, running off with it through the park railings and into the bushes at the back of the mortuary building, with me in hot pursuit. Sure enough, in the bushes behind the mortuary were the three pieces that had gone missing. The fox seemed to be using the leather as a chewing bark – or perhaps he could taste the horse in it. I decided that this was the last piece of leather the horsedrawn carriage was going to lose. I retrieved the old bits to see whether they could be repaired and put all the leather inside the back of the carriage to make sure that the fox could not return to repeat his actions. No wonder they call foxes crafty. If he comes back again, it will be to arrange his own funeral, I promise you.

And what of my own passing? Some might say that, for me, dying might be a kind of career move. If I were lucky enough to get to Heaven, what would I be given to do? If nobody dies there, I will be completely redundant. I'll have to have a change of career. I suppose I could always write books, but then I would have to find a new subject to write about. But even if I do face unemployment in a future life, I will know that my profession on earth has been a wonderful gift, and for now I will carry on my fight against bereavement wherever it raises its head.

How, in simple terms, can I describe the work that I do as a funeral director? I like to describe it as 'rocking the cradle'. All babies cry, for lots of reasons – sometimes to be changed, sometimes because they are hungry, often because they just want attention. But when a baby is in despair or in pain, the cry is very different. And what do we as parents do in our despair for that child? We rock the cradle, don't we? We continue to rock the cradle in the hope that, even in pain, the baby will sleep, giving the pain a chance to ease. As a funeral director at a funeral, that is what I see myself doing – 'rocking the cradle' of people who are in such obvious pain and despair, to try to soothe away that pain and ease that despair. To try to get them through.

And what of faith? For every great invention that man has known, someone has had to take a leap of faith. We are always asking what happens when we die. Do we become someone else? It would be quite something if our souls continued in some other earthly form. Millions of people die in the peace of their faith and religion, but is life far simpler than that? Balancing truth, good and evil can come down to a simple battle of nature. Is disease the real enemy, the evil, Hell itself, and health the ally that we constantly seek? Is existing for the best of our ability and luck the only real Holy Grail? Does everything really come down to something that simple? Is faith merely a comfort zone that we adopt through the worst moments of our life? Let's think about this. What is our purpose? Reproduction? Eating? Grooming? Simply surviving for as long as possible? Are these the only things that make any difference? Yet we reason, of course, so does that allow us to balance our time? Are we really talking about consciousness/self-awareness, and, with reason, did that evolve in us through nature? And how then might consciousness/self-awareness have evolved?

If you look at the cycle of the common caterpillar (as

one regularly does, of course!), most live their short lives in bushes or in trees edging themselves along the stem of leaves and twigs, looking for healthy green leaves to eat. Not having good sight, caterpillars use their front sensors to feel for another twig as they reach the end of their current one. However, if they do not find a new twig to continue their journey, they turn around and come back again.

Now think about this. Imagine you are holding, at one end, a twig with a caterpillar walking along it. When the caterpillar reaches the free end, it will use its front sensors to look for the next twig, but it will not find one. So it will turn around. If you then hold the twig at the other end, the caterpillar will again find nothing to climb on to, so it will turn round again. In theory, the caterpillar could do this all day until it became totally exhausted, without ever realising that anything was wrong. So did consciousness/self-awareness start in a part of an animal's brain that could actually recognise, for want of a better word, that activity? A caterpillar equipped with such knowledge would quickly realise that something was wrong, stop, think and be able to change its strategy, maybe just by letting itself drop from the never-ending twig to something below. We, as humans, though, are equipped with that ability in our reasoning powers.

You are probably thinking, 'Why's Barry speaking all this scientific twaddle?' Well, that's thanks to the questions and writings of my cryonics friends, the publishers of *Longevity* –

it really does make you think, you know – but I think that if we absorb and think about these things, our understanding of life as a whole becomes greater. Our awareness will be far more precise and our appreciation of life and death a little more practical. Perhaps, most importantly, our appreciation of consciousness/self-awareness, and our respect for our own and others' consciousness/self-awareness, will be better understood and served.

How typical of this profession that, just as things were getting a little bit too heavy here, the postman arrived with a parcel from the National Association of American Funeral Directors. I must just tell you what was inside: a small gift from them to me as President of the World Association of Funeral Care (FIAT/IFTA). It is a little set of silver cufflinks and matching tie-pin in the shape of an American casket. When on earth am I going to wear those? The only possibility is the Undertakers' Ball, and even then they would think me very strange. In two of the pieces in the set, there is a little golf putter, with an end in the shape of a casket and the words 'Your Rest Assured Golf Putter'. That would go down well on the golf course. Not that I go there – the holes I work with are at cemeteries. No par for the course there, although I have had the odd hole in one. Yet again, laughter is never far away in our profession, with no disrespect whatsoever.

So, in conclusion, when we say 'Death is nothing at all', deep inside we really mean the opposite – bereavement is our lifelong enemy. What the opening poem of this chapter tells us, though, is that the dead never leave us. They are eternally here, somewhere very near, just around the corner, so remember that all is well.

2

THE AFTERLIFE

People say that we go to church at least three times in our lives: when we hatch, when we match and when we despatch. And what then? Is there an afterlife? If there is, is it connected to religion? I believe we should always ask questions about life. My personal faith gives me the answers, but is there more? If there is a Heaven, I suppose there has to be a Hell. If there is a Hell, is it merely a place with the impossibility of reason, or is it being able to see something wonderful and yet never be close to it? If so, is Heaven the opposite to that? Is that wonderful thing God, or is it far more simple, in that Heaven is something we spend our whole lives striving for and Hell is this life itself? Could Heaven be a kind of tradition that we all hold dear from generation to generation? I have often felt that in my life and my professional work, holding the historical mantle of F. A. Albin & Sons, the very hardest part is being the living extension of a tradition. This itself poses a question for me: if I did not exist, would that in itself be the end of the historical continuation of that very same tradition? Or am I talking rubbish again?

Spooky things do indeed happen. One of the light bulbs just blew in the office where Joanna is typing this for me. As Jonathan got up to change the bulb, it came back on, and at the very same time the air-conditioning unit in Laura's office came on even though the control panel was still in the drawer and had not been touched. Very odd, bearing in mind that the electrics here are new and in perfect working order.

I have always held dear my belief that we should not hold testimony against the dead as they can no longer defend themselves. Or can they? The body certainly can. The remains of the body can still, for example, tell forensic scientists so much. Perhaps that is where the saying 'open up a can of worms' comes from. Many crimes have been solved purely using modern forensic science. Does the body reap its own revenge on the living who have offended it? It is an interesting thought that the actions of a person in life can be often answered for us in death. In this way, death could in fact be viewed as not being the ultimate end (for either body or soul).

There are, of course, so many stories and tales relating to the possibility of afterlife for the soul. For me, I am sure that all does not end with death. What I have been able to learn of this life is that there is so much more, and I think I have often made those feelings clear. When I look at somebody who has died and think deeply about all they have seen and experienced in their lives, and the people they must have touched in good and bad ways, those they loved and those who have loved them, I cannot imagine that all this is gone in one brief moment because a piece of apparatus, which is after all what our body represents, has finally broken and cannot be physically repaired or fitted with new parts. The pump that is our heart can no longer work, but is that really the end of everything? Are all those wonderful things brought to an end because of that instance? In my reasoning, that seems impossible: there must be, and is, I believe, more, much more.

If our television tube breaks while we are watching, does that mean that the programme is at an end? No, the apparatus is merely broken. The programme goes on and in thousands of homes, all around us, people are watching the very same programme. I have often suggested in eulogies I have given that, for me, the soul lives on, but we all need to see it to believe it – we are, as human beings, so curious and mistrusting.

In some of my eulogies, I have said, 'All around me now, at this very moment, there are thousands – no, millions – of voices. They are all around me and I know they are here. Do you believe me, or do you think I am mad?' People tend to look at me a bit uncertainly, so I ask them, 'Would you like me to prove it to you?' They usually begin to think anxiously, 'Ahh, at last we are going to have some proof here' – I can see it in their eyes and their nodding heads.

'Right,' I reply, 'all I need to prove it to you is a *radio set* with a receiver – switch it on, tune it in, and as I go along the scale I can pick up voices from everywhere. You see, those radio waves are continuously around us, containing thousands and millions of voices. Although we can't see them, we know they are there. Yet if we never had a radio receiver and if there were never a transmitter by which they could be sent, we could never receive them.

'For me, the body is both a transmitter and a receiver; we transmit constantly but are not always willing to receive. So I clearly believe that there is, after death, still much for us to receive from a person who can no longer verbally communicate with us. They can still connect with us and often do so in very simple ways, maybe from pre-death communications. It could be just a feeling sometimes, a warmth, a glow, a contentment, a moment in loss when we realise that we are not alone. Sometimes it is a small kindness shown by somebody not even close to us that relates to a kindness shown by the person we have lost, reminding us directly of them. If you have lost somebody very close to you, you will understand what I mean by this. There are those too who claim far more than just a simple feeling that someone is for ever close to them. Some have heard, seen or experienced far more. I may not always understand, but I never doubt.'

One lovely lady told me that her husband visits her. She regularly sees him standing at the foot of her bed just smiling at her, making her less afraid. Another woman said she often feels her boyfriend, who has died, touching her and whispering gentle words to comfort her. She never actually claimed to see her boyfriend, but the presence of his voice, and even the feeling of his touch, was constant. Seeing somebody you have lost or hearing their voice is not a commonly reported occurrence, yet it is quite common for people to say that they smelt somebody close to them, felt their warmth or found something belonging to them at a crucial moment in their bereavement.

These experiences usually seem to last for only a few months, but for some people they can go on for many years and become a source of great comfort. Many of these experiences have been professionally researched in surveys. In one survey, over 50 per cent of widowed people had had some experience of those they had lost, mostly a feeling of warmth or sensing a presence. We are not talking here about people who have been to a medium or have tried to contact the dead in that spiritual way. No, for these people things just seem to happen spontaneously – usually when they least expect it. These are ordinary people with normal lives, and interestingly it happens to both men and women on an equal basis, although I personally feel that women are more able to speak about it than men are. I believe that people who have had such experiences tend to cope better with bereavement than those who have not.

I honestly do not believe that these are just tricks of the mind or the memory creating illusions; I believe they are an extension of the person who has died, feelings that we are still receiving that have previously been transmitted. In one of my previous books, I mentioned my belief that a person's soul sometimes does not know they have died, and does not quite know how to leave at that point. Maybe these experiences are connected to that, or maybe the soul, such a treasured and precious gift that we have all been given, moves on far more slowly than we believe and goes on existing around us. Maybe it is the soul rather than the body itself that is the transmitter, which is why all does not end here.

In religious faith, we are born, pass through this life and pass through death to a new life. In the Christian faith, Easter is the celebration of just that. After all, the Bible says that Jesus passed from this life to the next, and in the weeks that followed his death he appeared to many people – all those who loved him. Is this then showing us how those contacts were in some way similar to our own after-death contacts with loved ones? We can ask all these questions because death is the biggest mystery to every human being. I have always believed that our uncertainty is about the journey, not the final destination; that is what we human beings are truly afraid of, along, of course, with thinking that this world can and will go on without us. Nobody in the world has the real answer, so maybe fear, and not death itself, is the real enemy. As I have said many times, we need to address this fear and then get on with our lives, putting death where it belongs – right at the end, and not before.

What I cannot and will not subscribe to, however, is the

thought that Christ could appear in the knot of a £46 pine door, headlined in the press as 'Doorway to Heaven', and at Easter too – very convenient, if you'll excuse my flippancy. It seems that this guy in a DIY store found the face of Jesus in the knot of a pine door. The gentleman in question happened to be a committed Christian, and seemingly a good businessman too, I am thinking, but to be truthful that kind of thinking really does not wash with me. How about you?

Now a little light relief from my seriousness in this chapter. I heard of a man who was offering his soul, in good condition, no serious damage, hardly used, and would you believe it on the Internet auction site eBay. Interested? He was offering it for £6.00. Make a nice Christmas gift, wouldn't it? He will even give you a soul number to go with it and, if you are really good, a guarantee. People can be so strange. There was a second soul on offer on eBay, too, this time from a woman in Devon. Her soul was actually bid for and raised an incredible 55p. It's obviously not in such good condition as the first one. Perhaps she suffered a lot in life. I really like human beings who have suffered as they are generally much kinder in life. Anyhow, no more soul-searching – or should it be soul-surfing? Let's move on.

Now, I may not believe that Christ's face has appeared on the knot of a £46 pine door, but I do believe in spooky things and have certainly experienced some inexplicable events in my life around my work, particularly relating to the bereaved. Around two years ago, I cremated the husband of a local Bermondsey lady. Both of them had lived their whole lives in the vicinity of St Mary's Church, Rotherhithe, which is in St Mary Church Street just next to the Mayflower pub. There has been a church there for over a thousand years, this being the church where the captain of the *Mayflower* worshipped and from where the boat left, first for Plymouth before the Pilgrim Fathers voyaged to the Americas. In more recent times, the local minister, Reverend Nicholas Richards, or Father Nick as we know him ('the pie and liquor' for all you cockneys), a colourful local character, has created a small cremation plot in the garden at the front of the church. Many people have worshipped at the church and have an affinity with it. They have had their ashes placed there in that garden with a little plaque, a lovely touch.

So this local lady, Sylvie, had her husband Tom's ashes buried in that ground, and in the middle of the ashes she placed her husband's wedding ring. Some two years later when she visited his plaque, there lying on the surface was his wedding ring. No ashes, no ground disturbance, just a wedding ring. I can see no logical reason how this could have happened without some ground disturbance or obvious clues, and to Sylvie this was an obvious message that Tom had wanted her to have his ring back. Now she wears it on a gold chain around her neck just as she believes, and I believe, Tom would have wanted. Strange but true.

Another brave lady, Helen, who lives not far from our

Mottingham shop, has recently become a minister. On the day of her ordination, in the late evening, her dear husband passed away. They had been joking days before that now she was a minister, she would be able to conduct his funeral. She had of course retorted, 'Well, I might go before you,' but he had assured her that would not happen. Did he have some premonition of his death? Who knows? His funeral was indeed Helen's first, but it was something she bravely saw as a real privilege, a special gift God had granted her. On the day, she was, as would be expected, very nervous and emotional, but her faith carried her through and she presented a wonderful tribute to her husband's life, a life they had shared for some forty years. Helen, too, sincerely believes that her husband has not really left her and feels able to talk with him and share her future life with his comfort never too far away.

We can, of course, occasionally leave messages from the 'dark side', as some people call it, before we leave this life. All right, it's actually through epitaphs, on headstones perhaps, but the 'dark side' sounds far more interesting. So how about the following:

- I told you I was sick.
- The bloke next to me isn't dead.
- You're standing on my face, moron.
- Nobody would read my books but everybody reads this rock on my head (good one for me).
- (A little spooky this one) See you soon.

- (How about) Get your dog away from my headstone.
- Room for one more.
- They say you can choose your friends but not your relatives. I'm surrounded by them.
- Remember me as you pass me by, for as you are now, once was I. As I am now soon you will be, so be prepared to follow me (actually on a stone somewhere, so my dad said!).
- Room for one on top here – I've never been so happy.
- Now get me out of here, it's not funny any more.
- I knew I shouldn't have had that last drink.
- I'm an optimist and so far not bad at all.
- Not dead, only sleeping.

I guess you would have to be quite brave to have any of those on your headstone – they are all a bit flippant, a bit tongue in cheek. But if you can smile at one or two of them, they have served their purpose. Laughter kills so many ills, and tears refresh the soul.

As a lovely lady I had never met before said to me when I was conducting a funeral with our fleet of Daimlers in Braintree, 'Sir, your livery is quite splendid.'

'Thank you, madam,' I replied, thinking to myself, of course, 'my kidneys aren't doing too bad either.' This dear and very proper lady was simply commenting, in a very old-fashioned way, on how nice our cars were. How lovely! I was so proud at the time. If I had been made of chocolate I would have eaten myself, I really would.

But I digress. We were talking about epitaphs. What do the symbols that we engrave on gravestones mean? What do they represent? Have you ever really thought about it? Well, here are a few for you to think about – some nurtured from Christianity, of course, some from superstition, some I guess just for the sake of art, but they all seem to have an old meaning of some kind and can still be found in graveyards all over the country.

- an anchor – meaning steadfast hope;
- an anchor and Bible – meaning faith, hope and charity;
- angels – messengers between God and man;
- birds – meaning the soul;
- a bunch of grapes and an ear of corn – meaning the blood and body of Christ;
- a cherub – meaning divine wisdom and justice;
- a cross – meaning Christ's suffering and a belief in Christianity;
- a cross, crown and palm – meaning trials, victory and reward;
- a crown – meaning reward and glory;
- a dove – meaning a symbol of God the Holy Spirit;
- an eight-pointed star – meaning regeneration;
- fruit and a vine – meaning the personality of Jesus Christ;
- ghouls – meaning deliverance from grief;
- the Holy Bible as an open book – meaning perfect intelligence and an acceptance of Christianity;

- an hour-glass – meaning time and its flight;
- the letters I.H.S. – meaning Jesus, saviour of humanity;
- ivy – faithfulness, memory and friendship;
- laurel – meaning victory and glory;
- a lily – meaning purity and resurrection;
- a mermaid – meaning the dualism of Christ, who is both God and man;
- a nine-pointed star – meaning the fruits of the Holy Spirit: love, joy, peace, suffering, gentleness, goodness, faith, meekness and temperance (in other words, I suppose, self-control);
- an oak – meaning strength;
- palms – meaning victory and martyrdom;
- a passion vine – meaning the crowning event in the life of Christ;
- a peacock – meaning eternal life;
- a poppy – meaning sleep, hence death since death is sleep;
- a rooster – meaning humanity's fall from grace and subsequent resurrection (I've never seen this);
- a shell – meaning birth and resurrection;
- a six-pointed star – meaning the Creator;
- a square – meaning life and earth;
- a triangle – meaning truth, equality and the Trinity.

Colours have their meanings, too.
- Black, I know, comes from the superstition that it is the only colour you cannot see through in the spirit world.

- White for purity.
- Red for divine love.
- Violet for suffering.
- Yellow for the goodness of God.
- Grey for penance.
- Black and white together for humility.
- Blue for truth and constancy.
- Green for an open victory.

Interesting, aren't they? All created by people, of course.

Epigraphs are not the only way of communicating information when it comes to death. What about the following?

SECOND-HAND COFFIN FOR SALE.
THREE PREVIOUS OWNERS:
DRACULA, OLIVER TWIST AND
FRANKENSTEIN.
BARELY SLEPT IN.
FULLY FITTED AND LINED THROUGHOUT
WITH SILK SIDE SHROUDS. ALL AMENITIES
IN GOOD CONDITION.
£100 OR NEAREST OFFER.
APPLY APOLLO THEATRE WESTFIELD.
FIRST COME FIRST SERVED.
(DEATH NOT ESSENTIAL BUT THE DEAD MAY
APPLY.)

Light-hearted good humour, obviously from an old theatre clearing out some of its better-used props! Less appetising, though, was an advertisement recently placed by a TV company who, very macabre, wanted a person who was close to death who would allow them to undertake a scientific experiment in front of the cameras (after death, of course), dissolving their remains to the original carbon base so that they could be shot into space, where the programme was suggesting we all came from. Whatever next? Believe it or not, shortly afterwards I read an advert in a magazine advertising for another person close to death. Another TV company wanted to film that person's body from the moment of death throughout the process of deterioration, explaining what was happening at every stage through putrefaction and dehydration all the way down to nothing being left but a skeleton.

How can this be television? What kinds of mind are asking these questions and wanting to see these things? In some ways, these are the spookiest of all things. Not funny in any way but very sad, I think, and disrespectful to the dead and to the sacredness of the body itself. I am all for freedom of choice, but to me this goes too far, crossing the line into offensiveness.

Talking about crossing the line to offensiveness, I heard about a man up north who, it is alleged, murdered his mother-in-law and may have sold her to customers in his butcher's shop or put her into curries. I pray that this is not true. The man claimed that he just ('just', if you don't mind) put parts of her in bins along the curry mile of the area, but there were alleged to be traces of her blood in his butcher's shop. I can't imagine a less respectful and more macabre departure. One feels that the horrors of this life could not be equalled, but I must have more faith in humanity. However, hearing about such macabre behaviour does make you wonder.

I am going to leave you for this chapter with a poem I came across by an unknown author – quite Christian and very sentimental in parts, but comforting too and refreshing after the story I have just told.

To my dearest family and friends, some things I'd like to say,
Though first of all to let you know that I arrived OK.
I'm writing this from Heaven. Here I dwell with God above,
Here there's no more tears of sadness, here is just eternal love.

Please do not be unhappy because I am out of sight,
Remember that I am with you every morning, noon and night.
That day I had to leave you when my life on earth was through,
God picked me up and hugged me and He said, 'I welcome you'.

'It's good to have you back again, you were missed while
    you were gone,
As for your dearest family, they will join us later on.
I need you here so badly, you're part of my great plan,
There's so much that we have to do, to help our mortal
    man.'

God gave me a list of things that He wished for me to do,
And foremost on that list . . . was to watch and care for
    you.
And when you lie in bed at night, the day's chores put to
    flight,
God and I are closest to you . . . in the middle of the
    night.

When you think of my life on earth, and all those loving
    years,
Because you're only human, they are bound to bring you
    to tears.
But do not be afraid to cry – it helps relieve the pain.
Remember, there would be no flowers unless there was the
    rain.

I wish I could explain to you all that God has planned.
If I were to tell you, you would not understand.
One thing is certain, though my life on earth is o'er,
I'm closer to you now than I ever was before.

*There are rocky roads ahead of you and many hills to
 climb,
But together we can do it by taking one day at a time.
It was always my philosophy and I'd like it for you too,
That as you give unto the world, the world will give to
 you.*

*If you can help someone who's in sorrow and in pain,
Then you can say to God at night, 'My day was not in
 vain.'
So now I am contented . . . that my life was worthwhile
Knowing, as I passed along the way, I made somebody
 smile.*

*So if you meet someone who is sad and feeling low,
Just lend a hand to pick him up, as on your way you go.
When you're walking down the street and you've got me
 in mind,
I'm walking in your footsteps, only half a step behind.*

*And when it's time for you to go . . . from your body to
 be free,
Remember, it's not your going . . . you're coming home
 to me.*

This reflects in truth the epitome of my belief and
commitment to the battle of bereavement.

3

YOU ONLY GET ONE LIFE
AND DEATH

In my life, and in my work as a funeral director in the running of F. A. Albin & Sons, I have always tried to be a good leader – some might even say a dictator! But I have never settled for second best for myself, the firm or the families we serve, and the final command has to be clear. The more people an instruction goes through, the less chance that it will be correct by the time it gets to the person concerned.

Imagine the old story of being in command of an advance unit in the Second World War and sending the message, 'Send reinforcements, we are going to advance.' The order is then passed back through four chains of command, reaching its destination only to be interpreted as 'Send three and fourpence, we're going to a dance.' (You get my drift.) So my point is that having only one leader is often the best way because the more who are involved, the less organised, smooth and accurate the eventual message becomes. However, I do applaud and encourage initiative among all the staff – as funeral directors, having initiative is an essential part of our job.

My son Jon was recently conducting a funeral at Beckenham Crematorium and was helping the family from the cars. As he did this, one of our very young apprentices, Danny (we call him Dinkle as he has a brother called Perry working for us, whom we call Winkle – obvious, really), opened the back of the hearse. Now, the hearse doors are opened and held up by two shock absorbers, and amazingly, all of a sudden, they both gave up the ghost (no pun intended) at the same time, which meant the door on the back of the hearse would not stay up. Now Dinkle thought quickly and, being just over six feet two inches in height, stood perfectly still like a statue with the door resting on the top of his head. As his very dark hair matched the door's black paintwork, you could not see where his head met the paintwork. In truth, unless you stared inquisitively, you would not even have spotted what he was doing. As Jon approached the back of the hearse, he told Dinkle to get his shoulder pad on in readiness for taking the coffin from the hearse. Dinkle whispered from the corner of his mouth, 'I can't move, Jon.'

'Of course you can, come along.'

'No, I can't move, Jon – look at my head.'

As Jon looked up, he immediately spotted what Dinkle was doing. 'The door's broke, Jon. I can't move, I'm holding it up.'

Jon, of course, thinking quickly as he has been trained to do (and instinctively does, may I say), turned and said to the family: 'If you wouldn't mind, I would like to carry Mum into chapel.' The family were, of course, very agreeable with this, having become quite close to Jon in the few hours he had been with them. Jon then proceeded to take Dinkle's place while Dinkle stood still, knowing his role as a door jamb. When Jon came out of the crematorium, he congratulated Dinkle on his initiative and quick thinking – and the amusing result. How was that for improvisation on everybody's part?

This life itself is not a dress rehearsal for anything else. We only get one life, and most of us only get one death. There are, however, the rare few who are pronounced dead well before their time. For instance, at a hospital in Middlesbrough, a nurse recently met with an embarrassing situation when she informed a family that their mother had died at midnight. The family – the woman's daughter, son, brother and sister – immediately rushed to the hospital, only to discover that the nurse had mixed up two patients and Mary was still very much alive – as indeed she still is today, thank goodness.

Even worse than Mary's predicament was that of a lady who was pronounced dead in the hospital and taken down to the mortuary refrigerator. During the night there was another death on the ward, and the porters were asked to remove the second deceased to the mortuary too. As they were entering the newly deceased person's name in the register, they opened the fridge door looking for a tray space for the new arrival. As they did so, they heard a groan. Horrified, they ran from the mortuary to gather themselves together. On re-entering, they realised that the groaning was coming from the lady who had been placed in the refrigerator earlier. Thank goodness it must have been at the wrong temperature and, despite being pronounced dead, the lady was not actually dead. She was immediately taken to intensive care, where she eventually recovered. So, you see, maybe you could die twice.

If death itself has a design, a kind of natural plan, how do we know when it may have begun a chain reaction that will one day inevitably lead to our own death? That might begin with the simplest of actions – having one drink too many, staying somewhere longer than we should have done – thereby, unbeknown to us, changing events. Events that could in fact be the link to death's chain reaction and lead to our own ultimate end. Strange, isn't it? A small change to our routine could be the beginning of the end. Likewise, not changing our routine might have a similar effect, perhaps with a different end, but an end just the same. It sounds as if I am talking in riddles, but in these scenarios life and death are both fickle and narrow lines to walk.

If all I have just said is true – and my experiences in life, especially as a funeral director, bear out my theory – other people's actions must also have a huge part to play in the possible tragedy of death's chain reaction. We are, as they say, damned if we do and damned if we don't. We will never know whether our actions at any particular time have prolonged or shortened our time on this earth. Maybe I can sum up this marathon of thoughts in the following advice: analyse it, understand it and then put death where it deserves to be – at the end of life, whenever that might be. I say this again and again, because you can't knowingly change any of it, you truly can't.

I recently met a man who, two years ago, while still only in his late twenties, suffered a dreadful car accident that left him seriously disabled. He needs constant care, having almost had the one life we are all given taken from him, and certainly having had it left seriously impaired. This courageous young man is determined to make every minute of the life he has left count. He is, of course, going to receive serious compensation for his disabilities from the car insurance company – when he receives it, he intends to travel the world, with help from carers and friends, and see all he can experience in life, buying himself the comfort that he needs and deserves.

Another big decision he has made is that when his death eventually comes, he wishes to be cryonically suspended, which he has arranged through me. Everywhere he travels, he now meticulously takes the cryonic shipping case and all the equipment for him to be perfused before being frozen after death. I hope it will not be me, but my sons, in many, many years to come, who one day receive the phone call from somewhere in the world to organise this man's cryonic suspension; I wish this young man every opportunity to enjoy his life for as long as possible. Tales like this make you realise how lucky you are.

We all face the terror of death in many different ways. Some of us hide away from it, some of us deny it, others laugh their way through it. One saucy Bermondsey character by the name of Crimble laughs his way through every aspect of life, including death. He is a determined person. When he was a young boy, he would spend weeks with his little gang gathering up firewood and making big pyramid bonfires ready for Guy Fawkes' night. He would sit for hours just to protect them, sometimes not going home until nearly midnight – risking a clout round the head from his old mum – just to be sure no rival gangs set light to them before the day. He was – and still is – a real little rascal, but what a loveable and kind man he is.

Now this is going to sound very unkind, and a dreadful thing to say, but when he heard that his sister had breast cancer he sent her a note saying, 'Well, don't worry, Sis, it's not much to lose: they've not been very big throughout your life; they're not your best asset anyway.' After the operation, he went to see her in hospital and took her in half a bra as a present! But his action changed the horror of the situation for her, because straight away she saw the funny side of it and they both burst into laughter and ended up hugging each other. Just for a moment, Crimble had crushed the terror of that dreadful operation, making her see that it was unimportant to him that she had lost her breast, but very important to him that he had her still with him. It was his way of encouraging her to make the best of it all and showing her the way forward. Together, they got through it brilliantly. It may have seemed like a heartless thing to do, but he knew her and she knew him, and it worked for them both. Sometimes I think that we have to face adversity as quickly as possible in order to be able to surmount it. And surmount it we must, because every moment of life that we have left is precious.

Have you seen that vodka advert on TV in which the 'hero', a big ugly fella, chokes to death only to hear his own self-commentary after having been cremated, while his brother is taking his ashes on a last car journey? The guy who is dead narrates (I paraphrase): 'There I am sitting on the seat in the urn. Ahh, my brother really loves me. See what he is doing – taking real good care of me.' They arrive at the destination, a place called Gems where you can have ashes made into diamonds. So we witness the ashes being made into a diamond and the diamond being returned to the brother. The brother then hightails it to a pawnbroker's, where he receives a tidy sum. He never liked his dead brother at all – nice one! The diamond is bought by a beautiful lady who has it implanted into her tooth. As you see her smiling, a last comment is heard from afar, proclaiming, 'Who says beauty and the beast don't mix?' Not very tasteful but amusing, I think.

We were recently en route to St Patrick's Cemetery in Leytonstone to complete an interment after a church Mass. We always keep to the old superstition of never going through the Rotherhithe Tunnel (or any tunnel, in fact), so that no one is taken underground before their time. We were going steadily along to Tower Bridge on our journey. Crossing over Tower Bridge and driving along the Mile End Road, just as you pass Stratford there is a sex shop-cum-sauna with all the windows blacked out. Sitting next to my son Simon in the first limousine was Father Redstone, a very jolly Asian priest, a lovely character and really friendly. He said to Simon, 'Why have they made their shop so miserable? Why is there nothing in the window? No one can see what they are selling. Why don't they just open up the shop so we can all see what they sell? They will go bust if they keep this up. I would not buy anything from there.'

Well, of course, Simon knew exactly what the shop was and could not keep a straight face, but he also could not bring himself to tell Father Redstone what the shop really was, so he simply agreed, nodding his head: 'Yes, Father, silly isn't it?' Well done, Simon – professional tact to the end. Father Redstone enjoys life, and perhaps it is better that he does not know what he is missing in that shop – but every time we pass it now we cannot help thinking of how embarrassed he would be if he knew what they were really selling. I suppose it might widen his horizons even more!

We recently conducted a funeral in Bermondsey for Harry, who was a renowned shoplifter. This gentleman was never off duty, so much so that even in the summer he would wear an overcoat. Like a true professional, he was always prepared. When his mates came to the chapel to see him, one of them brought the old overcoat and, having cleared it with his family, insisted it was put in the bottom of his coffin in case he needed it where he was going. Bermondsey characters make your eyes water one way or the other, but I love them all, I really do. One of his friends said to me, 'Bal, you can expect a hearse full of flowers to be sent from Smith's and Boots; they are so grateful he is gone, I'm telling you, mate, they are ecstatic.' If you didn't laugh, you would cry.

Another old mate of Harry's who came to see him in the chapel was Putty – the Millwall kit man I told you about in my last book. He is a saucy character and, of course, a football fanatic like myself. On one match day the chairman, Theo, was talking to someone in the tunnel when Putty came along and said, 'Come on, you are in the way – get out of the way.'

Theo looked at him: 'Putty, I should have sacked you years ago.'

'Yeah,' Putty said, 'for what you pay me, you wouldn't get a Brooke Bond monkey.'

Theo, being a bit quick-witted, retorted, 'Yes, I could, Putty – I've got you, mate.'

Now if you are a football fanatic, you are a football fanatic, and you can't get away from it. Anyone who knows me understands how much I admire Bill Shankly and always will. It was reported that he had taken his wife to a Liverpool vs Newcastle Reserves match on the day of his wedding. When asked if that were true, he said, 'No, don't be silly, it was Liverpool vs Man City Reserves.'

Anyway, I'm digressing again. The point is that Putty was an old mate of our shoplifting corpse, and he said that Harry had been a real scream. It seems that, after a few beers, Putty and Harry had gone out for an Indian meal, not something they did very often as they certainly weren't connoisseurs of Indian food. Harry called the waiter over and said, "Ere, mate, I've forgotten my glasses and I can't see the menu. I was here fifteen years ago; can you remember what I had, mate?' Oh, my goodness. I never tire of hearing stories about Bermondsey people – they are endless and always very funny.

So while we are in the laughing mood, how about a few famous last words:

- Is this gun loaded?
- It's only a rash – nothing to worry about.
- Are you sure the power is off?
- Mind the car! What car?
- It's only a small fire; it won't spread.
- The chance of anything happening is ten million to one.
- Which wire was I supposed to cut? (Bang)
- I am sure these are mushrooms.
- Let it down gently now.
- No problem; it will hold both our weights.
- This doesn't taste right, you know.
- Nice snake.

- At last, we have made it to the top of the mountain.
- That's odd.
- Don't be so superstitious.
- What does this button do?
- They look like a nice group of lads; let's ask them the way.
- Are you sure those brakes are all right?
- This is easy; I've seen this done on TV.
- Don't worry, I'll get your toast out.
- It'll never happen to me.

Interestingly, I was recently reading a very old book that quite strangely gave the causes of death for one week in the year 1700 (times were so different then!). It went something like this:

- Died suddenly – 2.
- Death due to teeth – 121. (How lethal were teeth in those days?)
- Death by piles – 1. (What a dreadful end that must have been!)
- Death due to stomach – 2.
- Burnt by candle – 1.
- Death due to cough – 2.
- Death by fright – 2. (So you really can be frightened to death, then – interesting but also stupid.)
- (My favourite.) Death due to the following – went to sleep but did not wake up – 20. (Can you believe that

twenty people went to sleep but did not wake up!
Surely the death caused the not waking up, rather
than the other way round?)

- Road deaths – 15.
- Unknown – 2.

Thank goodness medical science has come on a lot since
then.

Now to address a very serious issue in our society. How
many of us, when we are afraid of dying, have said to
ourselves, 'Please God, what will it take to keep me alive?' I
am sure, in truth, that when we reach a certain age, all of us
do so at some time or another. That is how precious life is
to us. Even at our darkest moments, we try to hold on to it,
yet does there come a time in our life when life itself
becomes too big a price to pay and we crave for its end? This
then prompts the question of whether euthanasia is the
answer, or at least a right that we should all have.

Euthanasia itself is an issue in our society that refuses to
die. Like most of you reading this, I have not experienced
euthanasia first hand in relation to anybody I have known,
and although I have given the issue some thought over the
years, I have never really been able to come to terms with
it. At times I think it is beyond comprehension. Even
though I fully understand the arguments for and against it,
what I do certainly stand in favour of is that everybody has
a right to die with dignity and without pain. The big
question for me, and for many others, is: who makes that

final decision? If we are the patient, will we be in good, sound mind to make that decision? If we are not of sound mind, who finally makes that decision for us? Will it ultimately be a decision rested on the medical profession, and if that is finally the case, is that fair to the doctor concerned to have, in effect, to play God?

A very good friend of mine, Heidi, who lives in the Netherlands, recently brought this issue to the forefront for me when, after dinner at our house, she told me about her experiences with euthanasia. Her own mother had in fact had her life ended by euthanasia, which is quite legal in Holland providing that correct procedures are followed in relation to the patient, the family and a number of individual doctors who must consent. I had never really considered the fact that euthanasia was legally used and practised somewhere in the world. The sudden realisation that this was actually happening legally did, I have to say, chill me for a moment. The stark reality of some issues can be quite frightening.

I was naturally fascinated by Heidi's story of what had happened. I hope I have the details correct here, but it was obviously a very emotional story for Heidi to tell. Heidi's mother had been dreadfully ill with cancer for some three years, the cancer becoming terminal. She had come to a point in her life when she no longer wanted to live. There was nothing left for her to enjoy. She could not sleep restfully. She had no interest in eating, was not able to taste anything and mostly brought up within minutes the little she had been able to get down. She was in constant pain, relieved only by heavy doses of morphine.

Heidi's mother could see no point to her existence so called a meeting with her doctor and her family. It was unanimously agreed that they would all gather in her room the next day as a family, play her favourite music, individually spend some time with her, open a bottle of champagne and celebrate her life. Heidi's mother was given a permanent sedative in a drink that she freely drank of her own will, and over the next five minutes she gently went into a deep sleep that extended into death itself. Heidi told me that there were of course tears and emotion, but it was a warm and dignified way to say goodbye that was her mother's last wish. As she was telling us this story, Heidi – as well as the rest of us – shed a tear. It was one of the most moving and emotional stories I had ever heard.

Heidi tells me she would have no hesitation in choosing the same death for herself should the time come. How about you? If you had the choice, could you make that decision? More importantly, could you make that decision for someone you love? Some might say such a decision would imply that you don't love them at all, but I think that you would have to love somebody very much to be able to make that decision. Again, I do not profess to have the ultimate answer. I don't want to be the judge of anything, and perhaps that is why religion says that only God should make that decision. You could, however, ask whether God is ultimately making that decision, working through us. The arguments could go on and on for a very long time, and I doubt whether euthanasia will ever be law in the UK in my lifetime.

Whatever the answer is, that evening opened my eyes and my heart. Heidi, you are very brave – my Ambassador of Courage. If we go back to the theory I posed earlier in this chapter that, without even knowing it, our actions might often be choosing between life and death, would a Living Will be the answer, or at least the first step towards legal euthanasia in the UK? Time will tell, but this is, without doubt, a dangerous and delicate subject.

The late Bob Monkhouse, one of our greatest comedians, is yet another example of a person facing death with great courage after a long and painful illness. Towards the end of his life, he said, 'When I was young and I told people I wanted to be a comedian they laughed, but they are not laughing now.' Well, you are wrong there, Bob: people will never stop laughing. Although you won't live on in this world, you will live on through your films, books, tapes and records, and will, for years to come, be remembered. Laughter is the most enormous help at such times. We must never be without it.

As we end this chapter, let me leave you with something called 'Times End', which I heard read at a funeral by my dear friend Alan McLean, a poem full of life's celebration and good humour.

Times End

I can't quite decide,
When my time comes
To shuffle off this mortal coil,
When to have the funeral.

It is important,
As different times of the year
Mean different arrangements,
Different approaches to the shindig.

A Spring funeral,
With young, fresh life
Proliferating in the parks and gardens,
Seems like a fair exchange.

A Summer funeral,
Where everyone can wear sunglasses
And look cool and sharp
In their bright summer clothes (NO BLACK!).

An Autumn funeral
Amid the gold of a fading summer
Seems like a more poignant exit,
Somehow in keeping with the season.

YOU ONLY GET ONE LIFE AND DEATH

A Winter funeral,
Just to annoy people with the rain and snow,
My last little joke, as I won't care,
I'll be going up a nice warm flue.

Whatever the season,
As long as everybody enjoys the send-off
In a celebration of life,
And remembers me with a smile.

Fantastic!

4

UHAT UILL I LEAVE BEHIND?

As I write this chapter, sitting quietly in my office at 10.30 on the morning of Saturday 25 December 2004 – Christmas Day – I am yet again struck by the overwhelming importance that there is for bereaved people to be close again, sometimes just for a moment, to the people they have lost. I am looking out of the window at the beautiful row of holly wreaths that have been left in memory of so many who have died, and for whom Albin's Memorial Garden has become the keeper and protector of those memories. I switch on the TV and notice a programme called *Don't Drop the Baby Jesus*, obviously (ha, ha) taken especially for Christmas from the title of my own TV programme *Don't Drop the Coffin*. That lightens my thoughts for a moment.

So many people are here today, sharing grief with each other. They are helping each other to park their cars as ever more begin to pull up, and I realise clearly what this place means to Bermondsey. My pride overwhelms me as I feel tears building up inside. Some people stop for a moment to look at the collage of beautiful photographs along the fence that people have pinned up for Christmas. The Christmas tree is still beautiful and full of the stars from the Christmas Memorial Service. People light candles at the gateway in memory as they leave and wave out to me, wishing me a merry Christmas. Oh, how I desire to wish the same back to them, but I know the best wish I could give them is for a peaceful Christmas. In the chapel here, there are a number of people who await their own funeral and, today of all days, their families will want to come and be with them.

A few minutes ago, a lovely old gentleman came to visit his wife, whom he lost three or four days before Christmas: her funeral will not in fact take place until the New Year. He came in and asked whether he could sit with her for a few moments. It was my greatest honour to prepare the chapel and make him comfortable there with his wife. As he was leaving, it was clear that he was very lonely and very upset, and just wanted to talk for a little while, which I was glad to do. Some of the chat was idle and some about the funeral arrangements that had already been made and understood, but it was important to him to share them with me again and finally ask me whether I would be with him on the day of the funeral – again, something I am very honoured to do.

As he was leaving, he turned and said, 'I wish you a merry Christmas, Barry; thank you sincerely for opening up for us all today.' Again, I was humbled by his thanks. I squeezed his arm, looked him in the eye and said, 'John, I know this is the hardest thing you will have ever had to do, but you must take every moment you have left of this life, just as Lilian would have wanted you to do. She will never leave you – I can see in your eyes she never will – but you have got your two boys and they will be looking to you now. They will be worried for you, and they will want you close. And John, you have endless grandchildren who are going to want to know about Lilian in years to come, and you are going to need to be here to tell them. God bless, John; have a peaceful day. Stay together and come and visit us again tomorrow.'

'Can I really come again tomorrow?'

'Of course you can; Maureen will be here.'

'Beautiful, mate, and don't you be here too long yourself – get home to your people. Bye now.'

When we move on from this life, we leave many things for people. One thing we will always have is memories, because nobody can rob us of those treasured things. They must be passed on to our children, our grandchildren and onwards for as long as possible. In that way, the sacredness of that person who has gone, their life, their soul, their presence here on earth, will never be forgotten. For me, this, and not some legal document, is a Living Will. Something that will live on for ever. I am constantly reminded of how privileged I am to do this job and serve this community.

Another thing we are certain to leave behind is our body.

In the UK, nationally, 72 per cent of us are cremated and 28 per cent buried. In South London, the figures are probably a little more evenly balanced as there are a lot more burials than the national average, but whether burial or cremation is chosen, we still need a place to remember, which is why our Memorial Garden is so well used.

A week before Christmas, a lovely young girl came in her car to collect the ashes of her grandad, who had been cremated in November, just to take them home for Christmas. I think that was a beautiful gesture. The family has not yet made the final decision on where Grandad's ashes are going to rest (probably, though, in our Memorial Garden), but Grandad is very important to them all and it has got to be thought out properly. As Jackie handed the urn to the young lady, she was trembling and very nervous. She took her grandad's ashes in both arms and, as she thanked us, lovingly and gently pulled them towards her. Heading for the door, she stopped, turned and asked what she should do with Grandad in the car. 'I know it sounds silly, but should I just put them on the front seat and put the seatbelt around them?' she asked with a soft smile.

'That's just what I would do,' Jackie said, 'sounds perfect to me; whatever makes you feel comfortable.'

'Well, I think he would like me to do that,' she said. 'He was always telling me to put my seatbelt on when I was driving – I can hear him saying it now – so that's just what I will do. I just wanted to be sure I wasn't being stupid.'

And she drove very carefully out of the courtyard and

down the road, taking her grandad home for Christmas.

Some of my most loyal readers might remember, from my book *Final Departures*, my using the word 'atonement' or, as I like to describe it, 'at one moment'. Atonement – when all will become clear. Peace with ourselves. Complete forgiveness, because if we take anger and bitterness with us throughout our lives, it will destroy us and we will never have any peace of mind or peace of heart. We must be brave. We must never take to the grave things that we should share in life.

I witnessed this recently in a young man whose father, a lorry-driver, had left home many years before. As the son, Harry, put it, 'My dad left home twenty-five years ago when I was just ten. He went on the London to Grimsby run in his lorry. He stopped off at a guest house, took up with the lady owner and never came home.'

I sat there in amazement. Here was Harry sitting in front of me, now thirty-five years of age, having seen his dad only two or three times in that whole time but able to say, 'What can you do, Barry? Life's too short and I can't hold any bitterness. Dad did what he did. He was a man, nothing more, not a saint, but he is still my dad whatever he has done, and I am going to bury him properly, and I am going to pay for it. He left nothing, but that doesn't matter. Mum's not here any more: she passed away about ten years ago. I've got no brothers or sisters, only my own wife and children, and I am not going to inflict any bitterness on them, so I am going to say goodbye to my dad properly, put him to rest and we'll all get on with our lives.'

Now that is proper real atonement. What his dad did all those years ago, for whatever reason, hurt badly, but Harry was not going to allow that hurt to continue into his family and his own children. I have a great deal of admiration for his strength.

There are, of course, people who don't see it that way at all and actually reap revenge in other ways. Take the American lady I met, who had perhaps not had the best of lives with her husband. When he died, he left her, along with the house and car of course, the grand total of $20,000 to pay for the funeral. And she spent the whole $20,000 on the funeral – well, it was about $5,000 on the funeral and $15,000 on the memorial – yes, $15,000.

'Wow,' I said, 'what sort of a stone did you have for your husband for that sort of money?'

'Only three rocks,' said the lady.

'Only three rocks?' I queried.

'Only three rocks,' she confirmed.

'My God,' I said, 'they must have been big.'

'Not bad,' she said, thrusting her hand forward. 'About as big as these three rocks on my finger.'

I have heard of taking the pennies from a dead man's eyes, but this takes the biscuit. This colourful lady had decided to spend the legacy her husband had left for his funeral not on him but on herself. I suppose you could call that a form of atonement, or perhaps you would call it self-atonement. She certainly double-bluffed him.

As I finish writing this story, I am reminded yet again of

how worthwhile these few hours on Christmas morning are as Mrs Vaessen, a lovable old friend now, pops in to thank me for looking after her son Paul throughout the year and to wish me a merry Christmas, as she does each year. Paul was quite a famous football player, playing for Arsenal, but sadly died at a young age. Mrs Vaessen visits every week, and I could see how important it was to her to visit Paul on Christmas Day. Again, I am a little choked at the generosity of spirit she has and the fact that she took the time to come in and wish me a merry Christmas and thank me, though she was still clearly in a lot of pain even after many years. Just knowing that we were looking after Paul's ashes here in the garden was very sacred to her.

So when we die, what will we leave behind? And 'will' is the operative word here. Should we leave a Will? If so, how do we do it? Do we need a solicitor? Can we write it ourselves? What should we say? Will it be legal? Well, let's see if I can help you here. I have always had a personal interest in things legal – perhaps that's why I became a magistrate – and I certainly have no axe to grind with solicitors despite what people sometimes say or think. Solicitors are an absolute necessity. When things go wrong, or if you are intending to leave a very complicated Will or Trust, you should by all means consider seeing a solicitor, and I for one would not decry that for a moment. The majority of us, however, leave Wills in a very simple and straightforward way.

There is no need to complicate things, and the simple

secret is that we should leave instructions clearly and leave nobody in any doubt about what is required. This should be done on a Will form, on which all the information must be correct, and we must leave an appointed executor (or executrix if it is a lady), and date and sign the Will in the presence of two independent witnesses, who must also sign and write their addresses. Then, providing we keep that document safe, our wishes in death will be correctly adhered to. At Albin's, we operate a free Will service for local people and any of our clients and families, but if there are more complicated issues involved I will of course be the first to recommend a solicitor. My first suggestion is that a solicitor should act as an executor so that there will be no misunderstandings or complaints. Using a family member as executor can be nice but can also put them in a difficult position at times.

By the way, have you heard of the man who goes into the solicitor's and says, 'How much are your charges?'

The solicitor replies, '£100 for three questions.'

'That's a bit steep, isn't it?' retorts the man.

'Yes,' says the solicitor. 'And your third and last question is . . . ?'

Well, let's be fair, a solicitor has costs and overheads like everybody else.

I have been very lucky in having an old friend, Peter Cathcart, as my solicitor. He has served me, this company and my family so well over the years. I have nothing but admiration for solicitors, but with simple situations I can in truth help ordinary people every bit as well, and for many people it can be a little bit frightening going to a solicitor's office. You are probably laughing now and thinking that it can be a little bit frightening going to an undertaker's office! I won't argue with that, but I have probably got a familiar face and my clients may have dealt with me on many occasions over the years and just feel confident enough to come and see me. Offering a free Will service gives people a bit more encouragement to come and see what they should do, which is to make their wishes clear for the people they are leaving behind, because in truth what you say and do in life has an enormous effect on death. To me, having a Will is an essential part of life.

So, what should we say in a Will? At the end of this chapter is a list of the things to include and in fact a Will form itself. Hopefully, that should leave you in no doubt and may encourage you to go ahead and make a Will if you have not done so already. As I always say, you only have to do it once, and then you can put the thought of death where it deserves to be remembered, at the end of life and not before. As the years go by, you may of course have to update your Will from time to time, which you can always do by adding what is called a codicil to the bottom. Personally, I prefer to redo the Will completely, leaving no doubts or room for error.

Human beings are complicated animals, that's for sure. Likewise, we often complicate our lives too, which makes our final Will even more important. History bears witness to some very unusual requests in Wills over the years. Take William Shakespeare, for instance (there's a good Bermondsey boy for you – or so we like to say). William Shakespeare married Anne Hathaway in 1582, when he was still a teenager. She was a little older, around twenty-six, yet despite over thirty years of good marriage he left her only – can you believe this? – his second-best bed and other sticks of furniture. (Who got his best bed, then? That's what I would like to know.) Shakespeare went on to leave the remainder of his estate, in its entirety, to be divided between his two surviving children. Amazingly, he never had the level of wealth one might expect considering the plays he wrote. (Although whether he in fact wrote them is, of course, a bone of contention in the literary world.) But Anne did not hold a grudge. Who she left the bed to – and probably all the bedbugs – after she passed away has, however, been lost in antiquity.

Jane Austen was another great writer to have left very little upon her death. Although she had written such successful books, she died a spinster with no real love in her life other than that of her family, a sister and six brothers. In Austen's lifetime, none of her major works was published under her own name. She left a simple (which is enough) single-page Will, giving a small legacy to one brother and virtually everything else she possessed to her sister, Cassandra. Jane was only 41 when she died, and the world was robbed of further great works.

Over the years, a number of stories have grown up around

Wills and Last Testaments. Some are legends, some true, some exaggerated. Many, of course, have passed through me as a funeral director, and I'll recount a couple of them to you now out of interest.

It is said that a man called Jonas Gruber, who passed away in 1946, had previously written a Will stating that he was leaving everything to a cats' home. This Will had, during his lifetime, been seen by his six sons and his daughter, but upon his death the six estranged sons were so angry and disgusted that they decided not to attend the funeral (a big mistake). However, Jonas' grief-stricken daughter, who loved him dearly, did attend. After the funeral, Jonas' lawyer came forward with a later-dated Will stating that his entire estate would be divided between those children who had attended his funeral, and so it was – the entire legacy and complete estate went to his daughter.

Another wonderful story concerns a Spanish gentleman, a devout Catholic, who had stopped at the local church when he was visiting Stockholm, of all places. As the man entered, the church was empty except for a coffin containing the remains of a gentleman. Our good Roman Catholic Spaniard knelt gently for about forty minutes and prayed for the soul of the deceased. As he was leaving, he noticed a condolence book. At the top of the page was a note saying, 'Those who have prayed for the deceased should enter their names and addresses.' He noticed that he was the first to sign but went ahead and did so. Several months later, he received a letter from a Swedish solicitor informing him that he was solely to inherit the estate of a millionaire. The man he had prayed for was a seventy-three-year-old real estate dealer who had no relatives whatsoever; in his last Will (which had not been seen or read until after the burial), he had specified that 'Whoever prays for my soul in church gets all my belongings to be shared between them.' God really does move in mysterious ways.

Another tale about a final Will was told to me in a number of versions, one through some international news in a magazine, and another through some American funeral director friends of mine. It seems that, in 1995, a lady was proceeding on a long car journey and was desperate to find a 'rest room'. She came across a funeral home that had lots of cars parked outside and lots of activity. Thinking she could quietly creep in and visit the ladies' room to relieve herself, she parked and entered the front door.

As she did so, she was unexpectedly greeted by the funeral director, who asked which person she had come to visit. In her panic, she pointed to a room at the end and suggested that she was here to visit the person who had no visitors. Also in her panic, she wrote her name and address in the guest book as the funeral director had asked (the fact that she used her own name and address is quite a surprise, given the circumstances). The lady then proceeded to use the bathroom and left. Several months later, she received a letter explaining that a man called John Jones (true or false) had left a Will indicating that anyone who visited his body while he was lying in rest would receive the full sum of his estate, some $5 million. This lady, it turned out, had been the only visitor, so had received all the money. True or false, it's intriguing, isn't it?

As human beings, it would be unnatural for us not to want to leave some kind of legacy after our death. Something as simple as the world believing that you were a nice person can truly be enough, and what we leave to and within our children and grandchildren is also a legacy of great pride and importance. Have you thought about how you would like to be remembered? What sort of legacy will you leave to the world? It's not just property or money but love, because that is the gem of all legacies. Most importantly, don't die wishing you had said something particular in life. Have no regrets, mend all your fences, put things straight between friends and family, clear the decks, don't die with regret. Remember the wonderful words of the song, 'Everything I Own', written by David Gates, reputedly on the death of his father:

> . . . The finest years I ever knew
> Were all the years I had with you
> And . . .

> I would give everything I own
> Give up my life, my heart, my home
> I would give everything I own
> Just to have you back again.

And another great song for a father, this time 'The Living Years' from Mike and the Mechanics:

> . . . *I know that I'm a prisoner*
> *To all my father held so dear*
> *I know that I'm a hostage*
> *To all his hopes and fears*
> *I just wish I could have told him in the living years.*

So if you want someone at your funeral, say so in a Will.

Remember that making a Will is nothing to do with religion, so don't make a silly excuse like 'Dad's a Baptist and Mum's an alcoholic so I'm not sure what my religion is, so I can't be bothered to make a Will.' And don't go thinking that something sounds silly in a Will – however silly it may sound to you, if it is relevant, say it. Be sure you say clearly what your wishes are for your funeral. Make it easy for your family and your executor, and leave no room for doubt. State exactly what you would like – burial or cremation, or whatever is available at the time. Choose your music, choose your hymns, choose your minister, and choose your funeral director. Be clear, and if possible pre-arrange your funeral. That is certainly something for the future and the sensible way forward because those wishes should not be challenged. Also, if you pay for them now, they should not cost any more in fifty years' time – a good deal, don't you think?

If probate, or proof of Will as it is often called, has to be obtained, which is currently the case on any estate of a value over £5,000, my advice is definitely to arrange for a solicitor to undertake that probate. It is a long and complicated procedure. Losing somebody is bad enough, but we do not need these things to make it any worse. However meticulous we are in our lives, we all leave a number of things unsettled when we die. There are debtors and creditors to be sorted out, funeral directors to be chosen, probate registry, the Post Office, passports and driving licences, pension books to be cancelled, utility bills to be paid, bank accounts to be closed. There may be property to be dealt with, share transfers, pensions to claim, family to be considered, life assurance and of course the dreaded tax man. Even in death we leave many complications and ends to be tied up.

So, as I promised, here are a few pieces of information about making a Will, and the main areas for consideration. At the end, there is a list where you can write down helpful information for the people you leave behind, and finally comes a Will form. Now don't be shy, don't be afraid – make a Will. You know it makes sense. Isn't it a nice thought to be able to go into the next life knowing that everything is settled in this one? It certainly would be for me.

Preparing your Will: main areas for consideration

I have prepared this brief guide in order to assist you in making some important but necessary decisions when making a Will. It is in no way intended to be a definite document and should not be regarded as such. It is meant to be helpful – no more.

Appointment of executor(s)

In my view, this should be a solicitor or someone very responsible, as this is the person or persons who swear on oath to accept legal responsibility for administrating the affairs of an individual upon their death. Their duties include: applying for the granting of probate; paying all debts and funeral expenses (using money from the deceased's estate); the selling or temporary administration of property; completion of documentation and dealing with relevant life assurance, pension companies and/or employer benefit schemes; payment of all amenity bills; completion of documentation and returns to HM Inland Revenue and the Capital Taxes Office, and inheritance tax computations (where applicable); preparation of the 'estate account'; and correct distribution of the estate to beneficiaries or trustees, etc.

The executors accept a duty of care to ensure that the estate under their administration is maximised to the full value (that all due debts are called in, that allowances and entitlements are claimed, etc.). Should a mistake occur, they become personally liable for any loss. So beware – solicitors are best equipped to cope, believe me.

If you are married and each partner is considering making a Will, the most common and simple method of appointing an executor is that you each consent to be the executor or executrix of each other's will (or, as I have already recommended, get a solicitor).

Appointment of guardians
Guardians of children have many of the same rights in law as parents. Choose carefully, ensuring that you are confident in the guardians' ability to care and cope. Regard should also be given to the age of guardians and their financial position. And before you make your Will, don't forget to check with them that they are willing to be guardians if the need arises.

Property matters
One of the many recurring problems that arise when settling a person's affairs is that of property ownership (house, holiday home, land holdings, etc.). To avoid costly complications and possible delays in settling your property affairs, you should give due consideration to the way in which property is owned before your death, as a little forethought can go a long way.

My experience has shown me that many married couples have thought that the way in which they held their property meant each owned half. In the majority of cases, however, this proves not to be so. Under the Law of Property Act 1925, each actually owns the whole of it. Furthermore, the ownership of the first to die dies with them, meaning that the property passes directly to the survivor, and ownership cannot be dealt with under their Will. This happens in many circumstances where the property is mortgaged and had been bought with the couple as husband and wife. As such, the property will always go to the surviving spouse and no portion of it can be left to, for example, children or other family members.

Personal bequests

Make a list of your most cherished possessions and decide who is to have them. Then decide whether you wish them to have these items immediately after your death or only at the time of your spouse's death. Husband and wife or partner should not share a Will; instead, they should have what are commonly known as *mirror* Wills (Wills that are identical to each other). As I understand it, the law says that, in the case of a joint Will, the man is said to have died first if both partners are killed simultaneously, leaving the female intestate (without a Will).

I hope that this brief guide has helped you in your preparation and shown the importance of having a Will. There is no expense involved (or only little if you get a solicitor) and it is not complicated, frightening or tempting fate.

So there you are – thy 'Will' be done.

And here is the form to do it on ('He who dares, Rodney – he who dares!!!' as the highly comical TV character Del Trotter would say), so get it done and keep it safe! If in doubt, seek professional advice. All this advice is offered without prejudice, and it is a good idea to get your Will checked.

Helpful information for those we leave behind

Name . . . .
Address . . . .
. . . . .Tel. . . . .
National Insurance no . . . .
Occupation . . . .
Date of birth . . . .
Executor/Executrix name . . . .
Address . . . .
. . . .
House deeds . . . .
Bank details . . . .
Account numbers . . . .
. . . .
Insurance policy numbers . . . .
. . . .
Property . . . .
. . . .
Your wishes . . . .
. . . .
. . . .
Who to contact . . . .
Any helpful addresses . . . .
. . . .
. . . .
. . . .
. . . .

. . . .

Other information (names of people to contact, etc.) . . . .

. . . .
. . . .
. . . .
. . . .
. . . .
. . . .
. . . .
. . . .

A sample 'Last Will & Testament' form is included in the Appendix.

Finally, a parting piece of verse.

Remember Me

*The day may come when my body will lie upon a white
sheet in a hospital busily occupied with the living and
the dying.*

*At a certain moment a doctor will determine that my
brain has ceased to function and that, for all intents
and purposes, my life has stopped.*

*When that happens do not attempt to instil artificial life
into my body by the use of a machine and don't call this
my deathbed. Let it be called the bed of life and let my
body be taken from it to help others lead fuller lives.*

*Give my sight to the man who's never seen the sun rise, a
baby's face or love in the eyes of a woman.*

*Give my heart to a person whose own heart has caused
nothing but endless days of pain.*

*Give my blood to the teenager who is pulled from the
wreckage of his car so that he might live to see his
grandchildren play.*

*Give my kidneys to the one who depends on a machine to
exist.*

*Take my bones, every muscle, every fibre and nerve in
my body and find a way to make a crippled child walk.*

*Explore every corner of my brain, take my cells if
necessary and let them grow so that some day a*

*speechless boy will shout and a deaf girl will hear the
sound of rain against her window.*

*Burn what is left of me and scatter the ashes to the winds
to help the flowers grow. If you must bury something
let it be my faults, my weaknesses and all my
prejudices against my fellow man.*

*If by chance you wish to remember me, do it with a kind
deed or a word to someone who needs you.*

If you do all I have asked, I will live for ever.

5

DIE ME TO THE MOON

Funerals today are, thank God, a very personal and private experience. Each funeral can be individually tailored to a family's wishes, and I have to say that honestly anything goes. In this chapter, we can talk through some of the extraordinary things that people have requested for their funerals. It will certainly give you room for thought, one of my reasons for writing these books being that people will think about and question everything and, I hope, eventually feel comfortable with their own wishes.

Those of you who know me or have read my previous books know that my philosophy is clear – it is perfectly all right to undertake any kind of funeral arrangement providing that it does not hurt or interfere with the dignity and liberty of other people. We must always keep some kindness and respect in what we do, and never forget that the body is of course sacred. I would sincerely hate to see flashing billboards at football matches advertising funeral directors or the services they have available, or to see such tactless adverts on TV, or huge names of funeral directors on the sides of hearses. No, respect and dignity must be maintained. That is not to say, though, that there is anything wrong with a little humour.

We all had a little chuckle at Albin's when we recently came into contact with a funeral director in France. We had undertaken an exhumation here in London of a person who had been buried many years before, as the family had decided that they would like both her and her headstone to be taken back to Normandy, to be re-interred at the new family grave waiting in a local cemetery. After obtaining all the necessary documents from the Home Office and cemetery, and having agreed with the French authorities that the interment would take place in France, two of our Albin boys, Paul and David, both very experienced and reliable, set off on the slow journey across to Normandy. What they experienced when they arrived caused them to giggle, I have to say. The name of the funeral director was Pompes Funebres Sol (*pompes funebres* meaning 'funeral directors'), and across the front of the family Sol's offices it clearly said 'R. Sol'. Paul looked at David: 'R. Sol funeral directors; are they sure?'

Dave replied, laughing, 'Nah, they must be better than that, Paul.'

You may think that, being a French funeral home, they would not connect things in quite the same way as Paul and

David obviously did, but the first person to greet them at the front door was a lovely lady who was born and bred in Streatham, London. Now surely she knew better, but of course Paul and David, being tactful, carefully avoided the subject. The family turned out to be really nice people, and R. Sol to be good funeral directors. Interestingly, they were also a garage, builders, masons and ambulance service – a real jack-of-all-trades. The head man, who spoke some broken English, apparently looked and talked like actor Peter Sellers' inimitable creation, Inspector Clouseau: 'Ave you got za lissense for ze body? You ave to ave dat or ze law will be in touch wiz us.'

But I still think they should change the name. I mean, it's like writing to somebody who has just bought a pre-paid funeral with you, a cremation perhaps, and starting the letter with 'Thank you for becoming a member of our cremation plan, to which we offer you a very warm welcome', or ending with 'We look forward to seeing you soon' or 'Yours gratefully'. When you are a funeral director, what you say makes a difference. What you write is even more poignant, and people will pick you up on the slightest things (before you pick me up on the writing of this book, may I just say that I write it without prejudice and pleading insanity).

At many Albin's funerals in South London, and indeed at many funerals across the country, it has now become quite common, as I mentioned in an earlier chapter, to release a dove or a number of doves to symbolise the setting free of the soul. This is usually done at the end of the service, sometimes to a prayer read by the minister, sometimes to a few words said by the funeral director. The doves can be released from a small cage or thrown into the air by hand, a lovely way to bring the ceremony to an end. The doves usually fly around two or three times to get their bearings and eventually fly home. I was recently explaining this to an American colleague visiting the UK, and he said, 'Well, it has become very common in America to release balloons.'

'Oh yes, we've had that once or twice here too.'

'Oh no,' he said, 'it happens on almost one in three funerals.'

'Well, that's a high ratio. What happens?' I asked. 'If you let them go on a Monday, do they come back on a Wednesday?'

'No,' he said, not recognising my little joke, 'they don't come back; they just fly away.'

Then he suddenly saw the joke and burst out laughing: 'Nice one, Barry, I'll have to remember that.'

Then we exchanged a little banter on things you wouldn't want to hear while undergoing surgery – for instance, 'Sister, is this a hysterectomy or a vasectomy?' (ouch). Or how about 'Come back with that, you bad dog,' or 'Hell, I was paralytic last night, but a quick hair of the dog straightened me up this morning' (from the surgeon of all people). Here are a few more:

- 'Wait a minute, if this is his spleen, then what have we taken out?'
- 'Hand me that thing, err, what's it called, the thingy-me-bob?'
- 'Oh no, I've just lost my Rolex somewhere in here.'
- (From the surgeon) 'Stand back everyone, I've just lost my contact lenses.'
- 'Has anybody ever survived 500 ml of this stuff – I don't think I should have given him that much.' (A nice one from Bill.)
- 'I know this guy: he's been sleeping with my wife.' (What a mistake to make!)

Bill also told me about a lady who smoked sixty cigarettes a day throughout her life and was known to her family as 'filter tip'. When she died in America, she had a casket that was painted like a filter-tip cigarette, and was of course cremated. So her money going up in smoke during her life seemed to be paralleled in her final departure.

For some funeral directors I know in Berlin, the joining of Europe and opening up of the Eastern bloc has not been such a good thing. You can wait up to three weeks in Berlin for a cremation, and there seems to be an extraordinary amount, an insurmountable amount I am told, of paper-work. Some families have turned to an enterprising funeral director in the Czech Republic who is undertaking crema-tions for German families within a week for a lot less money. The Czech Republic crematorium also has, believe it or not, a hotel and restaurant where the mourners can be fed and stay overnight before going back to Germany. I am told that it is about a four-hour speedy journey down the motorway both ways, but I hear it is undertaking (or overtaking?) about twelve funerals a week. Could you imagine doing it all at the speed I conduct a funeral, very sedately and slowly going down the motorway? It would take me about twenty-four hours.

There is, however, one huge drawback for the Germans: there is no problem taking a body out of the country to be cremated, but under bylaws you are not allowed to import ashes into the city. But this enterprising Czech funeral director has, so I am told, found a loophole in the law for covering that one too. He simply mixes the ashes with a little earth, and because there is no law against bringing earth into the country, he describes the remains as 'earth'. Rumour has it, though, that the Germans are hitting back by putting a tax on every body that is taken outside city limits, making it less attractive to do this. It is a little like funeral wars. Can you imagine a country going to war over who cremates their dead? Sorry, a childish mood has overtaken me here. It's just that the stories and the things that real people do are so amazing. Can you imagine everyone going to all that trouble to save a little money or a few days? For what you gain in time and money, you lose enormously in dignity. However, as always, I respect people's right to choose. It's not for me, though, if you have to go through all that palaver.

As a funeral director, my responsibility to the family and to the deceased, and the sacredness of the ceremony, whatever kind of ceremony is chosen, is paramount. It does not matter whether a person weighs just five stone or fifty stone, like a client I recently helped. That person's dignity must be preserved to the best of one's ability.

After the TV show *Don't Drop the Coffin*, I received a letter from a dear lady who weighed just over fifty stone. Having seen the programme, she had been moved by the dignity we showed to a rather large person whom we took into church – we refused to put the deceased on a trolley but carried the coffin directly on our shoulders up the steps and into the church. This moved the dear lady greatly, and being of very poor health, she had one overwhelming fear at the time of her death – how people would be able to get her out of her bed and her home with some dignity and care. She and Jackie talked, probably for hours, over the next week or two about what could be done, Jackie trying to reassure her that we would do our very best to maintain her dignity.

Having put all her trust in us, she pre-arranged her funeral, saying exactly what she wished: that, upon her death, she would be taken from her home (not through an upstairs window on ladders by the Fire Brigade but by our boys) to our private chapel, where she was not to be viewed by anybody, and that she was to go with her family on the day of the funeral to a local cemetery near where she lived and would be buried in the ground with a simple ceremony.

Jackie of course assured her that we would completely follow her wishes. This sweet lady had formed a kind of friendship with Jackie and would ring up every few months just to pass the time of day and, with a little humour, assure Jackie that she had not lost any weight and was still there. On one occasion, the lady's husband phoned to assure us how much difference it had made to her knowing that she would be cared for so well. For me personally, it is reward enough to know that we have helped to lay that lady's worries to rest.

A week before Christmas 2004, we received a phone call from the lady's doctor, saying that she had only a day or two left to live. She had become terribly ill and he wanted to confirm that we would come as quickly as possible when she passed away. Sure enough, two days later he phoned us again, telling us that she had just passed on. He was a fantastic doctor, very thoughtful and kind, and assured us that he would stay with the husband and daughters until we arrived and all had been completed. He too had become very friendly with this lady after treating her over the years, and he reiterated the confidence she had placed in us.

This was a challenge for all the lads and for Albin's. We gathered together, and I told them the enormity of the situation and the care we must have for this dear lady. To a person, they wanted to take part in this removal, so we prepared our vehicle. We own this really wonderful piece of equipment, made by the Welsh company Mangar, which will lift up to seventy stone on air cushions with compressed air. You simply lay the cushion underneath somebody by tilting them a little, and plug it into the wall and into the compressor. The air then lifts the person upwards, each cushion rising to a very sensible level so that you can actually control the movement of the deceased. We also have a very strong steel tray and a beautiful ambulance with a hydraulic lifting system inside.

All things being ready, off went our big strong lads, honest and willing, with good strong shoulders. When the boys arrived, they settled the family down and told them that all would be well – it was just a matter of doing things slowly and with great care, and everyone had to be patient. The house doors had to be removed, as did the chair lift the lady had used for going up and down the stairs. With our marvellous air machine, some pulleys and a lot of goodwill, the removal was slowly completed over some four hours. Then we replaced the doors, put the chair lift back (the husband, who still uses it, told me it has never worked so well) and left everything clean and tidy, just as we had promised. We then brought the lady back in the ambulance and placed her into her own air-conditioned and cooled room while her coffin was being handmade to be extra strong. It was a huge casket and could only be lowered by twelve good men.

The cemetery was marvellous: they charged no extra for the grave even though it was twice the normal size, and the staff were so helpful. I personally conducted the funeral, which was completed to her family's total satisfaction, with the utmost care and in as dignified a fashion as possible considering the difficulties we faced. Jackie was very sad as this kind lady left the chapel that morning, but at least we had the self-respect of knowing that we had abided by her personal wishes.

The family of this dear lady kindly wrote the following to the *Telegraph* newspaper (I have slightly edited it to protect identities):

May I through your paper thank some wonderful people.

Unfortunately my wife died on the 23 December after a long illness.

First would be our doctor, Dr—, and Nurse—. They were both kind and wonderful and made the death of my wife so much easier than it would otherwise have been, she passed away in her sleep; I am so grateful to them both, their skill and expertise were of the best. Their manner to the both of us was so kind and gentle and made matters so much easier to deal with, the advice they gave was wonderful and of great help.

Secondly F. A. Albin's Funeral Directors London. My wife had many fears because of problems that she had, none of which were realised due to the way F. A. Albin's dealt with those problems. The expertise of the men of this firm are of the best, I cannot praise them highly enough. Our thanks to Barry and his sons, the

proprietors of the firm; they are very special people as
are indeed the men who dealt with my wife; they are a
credit to Barry in the manner of respect shown to my
wife and indeed to me. Special thanks to a kind lady
called Jackie who gave such security to my late wife.

Well done, as ever, my people. And well done too to the
cemetery for not practising sizeism, unlike a crematorium in
the north of England which instructed funeral directors by
letter (can you believe it?) to hold the cremations of fat
people only in the mornings and not in the afternoons. The
order came from council officials that any person weighing
more than nineteen stone had to be cremated no later than
9.30 a.m. because the ashes clog up the crematorium
burners. So funeral directors are being asked to calculate the
person's weight before the funeral is booked. How ridiculous
can you get?

Those in charge seem to know nothing about people,
bereavement, funeral directors or the profession in any
shape or form. They claim the bodies burn too quickly in
the afternoon, mainly because the crematorium furnaces are
hotter. We know that's true, but they say it creates too much
ash and blocks up the burners – so unblock them, and do
not victimise people because of their size. There are many
sometimes uncontrollable factors contributing to people's
size. Let's treat everybody the same and take the rough with
the smooth. It's OK, I suppose, if you are one pound under
nineteen stone, as you can then be cremated in the

afternoon. To me, this attitude is just the limit of insensitivity and totally unworkable. Those who hold such views would be better getting a job that does not involve care for others.

Let's change the subject. Why 'Die me to the moon' (a play on words, of course) for the title of this chapter? It seems to me now, having been a funeral director for the whole of my life, that almost anything is possible. It is a well-known fact that you can be cremated and have your ashes flown to the moon or, if you wish, just shot into space. In previous books, I have told you all about freeze-drying, cryonics, and even a lady whose husband loved her too much to let her go so sealed her in a coffee table in the living room. Do you remember that one? ('Have a beer on the wife, lads.')

Your ashes can be scattered just about anywhere today, and when it comes right down to it I guess that there aren't too many places where people cannot be buried. We can put ashes into a firework and launch you into the clouds, or scatter you from a plane down to earth. We can even put your ashes, as did an Australian lady, into her breast implants – ouch! We can have our ashes moulded to a coral reef to give fish a home for all time. We can be cast into diamonds. Made into paintings with ashes. Cast in pottery. Blasted into glass. Made into books. So today, if you can imagine it, it can happen.

I hope that regular readers have enjoyed the little stories from around the world that I have always included in my books. Funeral directors are a friendly lot, you see. If something strange or funny happens to us, we make sure that the rest of us know about it, usually via our magazines, some very obscure, from around the world. South Africa, America, Germany – most countries probably have a funeral journal. So I have put together for you here a few stories I have encountered over the past year or so. They all make me think, make me chuckle and sometimes make me a bit sad. I hope you enjoy them too.

The two burglars breaking into a house in France were startled by a corpse, but the noise of the break-in caused the neighbours to call the police. When they arrived, the burglars had of course fled, and it was later revealed that the corpse had been dead in that particular apartment for over four years. The neighbours had noticed the burglars rummaging around next door but they had not noticed the extraordinary quiet from the neighbour who had died four years previously. The caretaker of the apartments even had the cheek to say that 'He was a nice old man who had lived alone but rarely spoke to anyone.' You're certainly right there, mate: he didn't speak to *anyone* for at least four years.

A not too dissimilar story comes from Japan. The Japanese police reported that a dead man had been ignored by crowds on a busy street corner for over two months. He was found in front of a department store in Osaka, Japan (I've been there – a nice place). Can you imagine that happening in Oxford Street? Doesn't anybody ever clean the street in Japan? The man was reported to the police by a taxi-driver who noticed that the man had been there for some length of time without moving. It seems the body had even decomposed to a certain extent (maybe explaining why the Japanese wear those little masks in front of their faces!). How many millions of people must have passed him by? Isn't it sad? I don't know what the world is coming to.

In a nightclub in Canada, we had another similar case in which the mummified remains of a DJ who had been missing since October 2002 were found quite by chance between two walls after people complained of a bad smell in the area. The police said that no foul play was involved; it seems that the DJ had wedged himself between the walls (maybe as a prank) and had perhaps slipped and got himself into a position where he could not breathe properly, which caused his death. It seems that his family and friends, as well as the police, had been unsuccessfully looking for this gentleman for some time. All a bit freaky.

A slightly different case, but again involving somebody who had been dead for some time, was that of a man who stored his wife's body for over six years in his back yard in the hope that she could be restored to life at some time in the future. Probably having read about cryonics, he had wedged her upside down in an old freezer – in effect, a kind of home-made cryonic suspension. He must have been very much in love with his wife. He was alone and probably had no one to advise him better. The body was only found after neighbours complained about the rubbish around the outside of the house and a smell coming from the home.

When the police went into the house they found cabbage, old vegetables, newspapers, cat faeces, rats, everything you can imagine in such circumstances (hence the smell). That poor old gentleman needed help. He had, however, had the intelligence to use dry ice to freeze his wife, packing it into the freezer and shutting the lid tightly. Also packed in the ice were the bodies of ten cats. It was a well thought-out plan, but a sad situation.

In Malaysia, it seems that they are considering vertical graves – burying people standing up – to save space. This is not the first time that this has been done, but I am not sure that it would genuinely save space in the long run. When we bury people horizontally, we usually bury them perhaps as many as four deep in a family grave so, for the length of one coffin, there could be four family members in the fullness of time. I am not sure you could dig down that deep for vertically standing coffins, but maybe burial plots are individual in Malaysia.

How about the last wishes of a steam-train fanatic? The steam buff died at fifty-seven years of age, his last wishes being to be cremated and have his ashes placed in the firebox on the engine of the Isle of Wight Steam Railway near Cowes. This was reverently done so that he could enjoy his last steam railway ride!

And what about the gentleman from America whose ashes were due to be scattered near his home in Oregon, but on their final journey on an aircraft (and don't ask me how this happened) they fell out, dropped through the roof of a house and wedged in the rafters in the attic. The poor lady owner of the house, who was working in the kitchen, commented, 'You thought the roof had fell in; it was earth-shattering.' Now that's what I call a very dangerous last descent.

A Dutch dustman who died wanted his coffin to be carried on his yellow dustcart to the cemetery, although the coffin had to be placed down into the yellow part of the dust-holder and protruded from the back. This was very fitting for the way he had lived his life. To him, his work was a true profession, and rightly so. Never be ashamed of the job you do or the clothes you wear to do it. Always have great pride in your occupation.

I also heard of two very strange requests. One came from a Dutch man who, after his death, wanted to be fed slowly over a number of years to the snails. I cannot confirm whether or not this was actually done but it was certainly what he wanted. A German lady who had read about this then decided that, upon her death, she would like to be fed to piranhas – seeing as snails would take much too long, and anyway aren't snails vegetarians? Surely piranhas would gobble you up a lot more quickly? Personally, I thought piranhas liked their food live rather dead, so that might cause a bit of a problem. These requests, I believe, cross the line: as they affect others, they are, to me, not acceptable.

Another recent report I read was on a funeral director in the Bedfordshire area, a rural part of England, who had converted a farmer's Land Rover into a hearse (ideal for four-by-four fans, that one). The results seem to have been very popular. Lots of brownie points for initiative to that funeral director.

All these stories just go to show that there is nothing stranger than folk in life or in death.

I am often asked to undertake eulogies at funerals, usually for families that I have known very well over the years but occasionally for someone whom I do not know at all, which means that I need to discover a lot about that person as quickly as possible. Not being the closest person, I am obviously not the best qualified for the job, but sometimes the closer you are to somebody, the harder it is to stand up at the funeral and talk about the person you love so much. Having done that myself, I know how difficult it is, and it is sometimes just better for someone else to do it for you. But that is a great responsibility and must be done well.

So how do I go about the task? Everything in life is really about preparation. I like to sit with the family and talk about the person who has died, their life, where they were born, where they grew up, which school they went to, their first job, where they met their wife or husband, all about their children and grandchildren, what they achieved in their lives, what they enjoyed, funny stories that may have happened over the years . . . Then I put them together like a life history. It's as simple as that, really.

When someone dies at quite an old age, I like to recall the fact that they were once young men or young women with hope in their hearts and wings on their feet, rather than thinking of them as always being old. You have got to look at when they were born and what was happening at that time. Give people a sense of atmosphere of what it might have been like to have been born in the 1920s, for example. What did things cost then? What were the fashions? Who was famous at that time? Always reflect a little bit on what life was like when that particular person was born into this world, and then travel through their childhood and up to the person that we knew them to be today. Properly done, a eulogy is a real comfort and something I immensely enjoy doing for people – a great privilege and a definite honour. I always like to end with a little reading, something poignant that people will reflect upon.

So now to finish this chapter, I am going to put down for you a few of the readings that I often use to finish eulogies. These were not written by me but by all different kinds of people. What they have in common is that they bring a good eulogy to a fitting end, just as I hope they will do for this chapter.

A Time for Everything

There is a time for everything,
and a season for every activity under heaven:
A time to be born and a time to die,
a time to plant and a time to uproot,
a time to kill and a time to heal,
a time to tear and a time to mend.
A time to weep and a time to laugh,
a time to mourn and a time to dance,
a time to scatter stones and a time to gather them,
a time to embrace and a time to refrain.
A time to search and a time to give up,
a time to keep and a time to throw away,
a time to be silent and a time to speak,
a time to love and a time to hate,
a time for war and a time for peace.

(Ecclesiastes 3:1–8)

The Ship

I am standing upon the sea-shore.
A ship at my side spreads her white sails in the morning
    breeze
and starts for the blue ocean.
She is an object of beauty and strength and I stand and
    watch until she hangs
like a speck of white cloud just where the sea and sky
    come to mingle with each other.
Then someone at my side says, 'There she goes!'
Gone where?
Gone from my sight . . . that is all.
She is just as large in mast and hull and spar
As she was when she left my side
And just as able to bear her load of living freight to the
    place of destination.
Her diminished size is in me, not in her.
And just at that moment when someone at my side says,
'There she goes!'
there are other eyes watching her coming, and other voices
ready to take up the glad shout
'There she comes!'

(Henry Jackson Van Dyke, 1852–1933)

You might also want to look up the following beautiful verses, which we are unable to print in full for copyright reasons:

- 'Do not stand at my grave and weep' by Mary Frye (1932).
- 'If I should go before the rest of you' by Joyce Grenfell (1910–79).
- 'The life that I have' by Leo Marks (1920–2001). Featured in the film *Carve Her Name with Pride*.
- 'Stop all the clocks' by W. H. Auden (1940). Recited in the film *Four Weddings and a Funeral*.

6

FROM THE STAFF'S POINT OF VIEW

The single biggest investment I have ever made at Albin's is reflected directly in the staff. The staff is its lifeblood and by far its greatest asset – which should be the case in any successful business. Without the self-belief of the staff, their selfless dedication, skill and care, how could Albin's be the company that it is today? Sure, it needs a good leader (which I hope I am), and yes, in my sons there are budding new leaders. Put this all together and we of course create an invincible team, but it must never be forgotten that we are dependent daily on each member of staff here and, most importantly, on everyone's goodwill. So how do you create that goodwill? How do you get people to sincerely believe that they belong to a family here at Albin's (or any environment)? How do you keep that going 365 days a year, twenty-four hours a day, seven days a week?

I think that the answer to this is simple – if the company in itself and through its management cares for you, you will automatically care for it. If the company respects you as an individual and believes in you and the work you are doing, you will likewise have the same self-belief in the company. I am fortunate to be able to say that, at Albin's, we have been able to create this kind of atmosphere. In fact, there is a list of people who would like to have a job with us. I am not being arrogant about this; I am truly grateful, and am always anxious that anybody new who comes to the firm is agreeable to everybody and not just me.

Any new employee at Albin's has to be met by all the staff, and the staff in general have to agree with that person joining the team. We have a way of working here, and an atmosphere, that I would not like to see change. We are all batting for the same team. Somebody who was not doing that would stick out like a sore thumb, and I am not going to allow that to happen here.

The staff at Albin's always pull together, and when there is a problem we face it together. When there is a natural disaster and people are required to volunteer for work that is beyond the call of duty, you see everyone's hands go up, not just one or two. A number of staff have regularly been involved with trips to Iraq, Afghanistan, Kosovo and such places to bring back soldiers who have been killed in action or sometimes by natural causes. As I write this, Christopher from our sister company, Kenyon Christopher Henley, is in Thailand heading a team of people who are arranging the repatriation of those killed in the tsunami of Boxing Day 2004. We have drivers who, at weekends and throughout the evening, are going to the airport to collect these people and take them to the Coroner's Office. Over Christmas and the holidays we run a twenty-four-hour emergency removal service for people who have died at home or in nursing homes. Our phones are constantly answered by staff, and we are always ready to respond.

Working in the funeral business is not an easy job. Being a funeral director is not just about looking after the dead and counselling the bereaved – it is about looking after the living, too – and every job you can imagine is involved in a funeral director's work. Cars have to be cleaned and repaired, coffins have to be made, fitted and polished, deceased people have to be embalmed, washed and dressed. Preparations for the funeral are enormous. Ministers have to be booked, churches, music, service sheets, memorial cards, condolence books, flowers, memorials. Traffic problems and navigation need to be dealt with. All these aspects of the work are combined with the normal processes of running a business – telephones, computers, premises, vehicle repairs and renewals, VAT, taxation, accountancy, banking, mort-gages, overdrafts, clothing for the staff (which at Albin's always has to be immaculate). The shuffling of paper, the ordering of materials and goods – you could go on and on. I think that what I am trying to say here is that there is more to funeral directing than meets the eye!

You also have to have a very good understanding of cultural needs and religious requirements across the scale. You could be asked to deal, on a daily basis, with the needs of Christianity and its various branches – Church of England, Baptist, Methodist, Roman Catholic, Free Church – Hinduism, Baha'i, Buddhism, Islam, Rastafarianism, Sikhism and of course not forgetting Humanism and many more. All beliefs have to be respectfully adhered to, and we must have a reasonable knowledge of all the necessary requirements and traditions.

So how does Albin's, as a company, look after its staff? One way is that I hope the staff believe that Albin's provides the opportunity of a job for life, which is no longer commonplace. We ensure that they have all the clothing that is required – garage wear, funeral wear, removal wear, garden wear – and all that clothing must be complete, all the way down to socks, warm garments and shoes. Whatever is necessary for man or woman, Albin's will provide it and always to the top quality available. A unique clothing design, using only the best available (except for the black socks, which, OK, I get from a Turkish man in a van!) is another aspect of Albin's success. The staff receive extremely good salaries, well above the average for their opposite numbers in other firms. They are well respected by the local community; in Bermondsey, being an Albin's person is really quite special.

Food is provided at breakfast each morning, and there are always biscuits and sandwiches around at lunchtime for anybody who wants something. Drinks are readily available all day long, and when staff are out for the full day on funerals, somewhere along the line there will be sandwiches and tea for them.

Health care is a major issue at Albin's. We have a company doctor scheme with our own doctor, Alan Campion, who regularly keeps an eye on the staff. They receive flu jabs if they require them, they have inoculations against disease, regular blood tests and examinations, and counselling if it is required. Each member of staff is also a member of a health-care scheme for private health treatment. There is a small loan club without interest. They receive legal help and advice from the company solicitor without charge. Financial guidance from the company advisor. Tax advice from Jon Fletcher, full pensions, full holiday leave, sickness pay and, I hope, overall family care. I hope that they feel they can look to me for help any time, and they certainly seem to.

I have a firm belief that all companies should treat their staff in such a fashion. It may seem like a huge step to put all these benefits in place, but at the end of the day I am well rewarded by the staff in their loyalty and attention to duty. Whether you are an apprentice here, a funeral arranger, a chauffeur bearer, a foreman, manager or, like my sons, directors and shareholders of the company, everybody is shown the same level of respect and care.

'Respect' is probably the key word here. If something goes wrong, as a team we try to put it right. If I am angry about something that has happened, my anger is always temporary. We bring the problem to light, deal with it, discipline staff if necessary and then forget about it. That is my policy, and that's just the way I am as a person. I think the staff and my family appreciate that. I may not be the easiest person to work for, but I hope I am the most caring. Some might say I am a dictator or a tyrant, but I'm sure I'm more of a pussycat, really – judge that yourself! I think, however, you can generally say that, at Albin's, we enjoy each other's company and get on with the work, which I truly believe to be a sacred task. The disposal of the dead, after all, is a corporate act of mercy and a great privilege.

I thought it would be interesting to ask six people who work at Albin's, a cross-section really – an apprentice, a funeral arranger, garage foreman, etc. – to write down a little bit about why they are at Albin's and what the job means to them. They were not chosen: I just handed the forms out indiscriminately. My sons and other directors of the company are not included, only the everyday staff who mean so much to us. Let's start with apprentice Danny Mulligan:

Name: Danny Mulligan
Age: 17
Job title: Apprentice funeral director
Why I am at Albin's: I am at Albin's because I am looking for a lifetime career and a responsible job.

Name: Paul Rutherford
Age: 37
Job title: Garage foreman

Why I am at Albin's: For a lifelong career and a *great* workplace to be involved in.

Name: Joanna Downes
Age: 34
Job title: Receptionist/funeral arranger
Why I am at Albin's: I was asked to come here by Barry after meeting him on a pilgrimage to Lourdes (deadhunted!!!). I have been here for nine years now. I work with lovely people – like a big family. Work is very fulfilling and I can't imagine being anywhere else.

Name: Gregory Mancini
Age: 25?
Job title: Operations manager
Why I am at Albin's: In 1994, I had to choose a work placement for school. My father asked Barry if he would take me on for two weeks. Strange as it may seem, I thoroughly enjoyed the work, and most of all the friendly family environment. The work placement led to me having a Saturday job and holiday work. After finishing college, I was offered a modern-day apprenticeship for three years. This year will be my ninth year full time.

Name: Mark Richards
Age: 25
Job title: Embalmer

Why I am at Albin's: As a local Bermondsey boy whose family have used the services of Albin's over the years, I am proud to be part of a team who are committed to the great job that we do. I look forward to the new tasks that I may be involved in and thank the firm for the support and training that I have been given. I know that the position I hold as senior embalmer carries a great responsibility and commands skill and an eye for presentation.

Name: Michael Thorpe
Age: 38
Job title: Funeral director
Why I am at Albin's: After almost twenty-three years as a funeral director, I have never worked for a firm like F. A. Albin & Sons. Skill, integrity, attention to detail and sheer professionalism, all of which is expected of a modern-day funeral director, are just small points that are of paramount importance at this wonderful firm. The staff are real characters, friendly, warm and so supportive to everyone they meet. And what I have discovered is that over the past years, I have had the privilege to be in some very high-profile funerals (Freddie Mercury, Sir Anthony Quayle, Earl Spencer, Field Marshall Sir Richard Hull, Willie Rushton and Sir Denis Thatcher, just to mention a few!!!), and I know that in my heart whoever should come through our doors at Albin's that person will be treated with

the greatest respect. That is why I am so proud to be part of a unique team.

I hope that perhaps briefly explains what it is like to be at Albin's. I didn't interrupt them or edit them!

We do a very serious job (deadly serious, if you'll excuse the pun), and it is important that, at private times, staff are occasionally allowed to let off a little steam – as they sometimes do at breakfast – and enjoy a little laughter to lighten the day. When you are conducting a funeral, what you say when you first arrive at the home often determines the mood of the funeral throughout, and people's reaction to you is very important. Sometimes the most harmless comment can be misinterpreted but then sorted out, leaving everyone with a touch of laughter.

Take my son Jonathan, who regularly conducts funerals. At a recent local one, he went up two flights of stairs and walked along the landing towards the door of the family flat. The door opened and two dogs ran out excitedly, jumping up to him, with the two sisters of the deceased just behind them.

'Good morning,' said Jon. 'Well, I've never been welcomed by two dogs on a funeral before!'

'Oh,' said one of the sisters to the other, 'that's charming! Did you hear that, girl – he just called us a pair of dogs!' (which in Bermondsey means not too attractive).

'No, no,' hurried Jon. 'I didn't mean you, I was talking about the dogs.'

But the girl immediately laughed and put her hand on Jonathan's shoulder. 'Jon, it's all right, we were just joking – it was really good you just said that.'

And from that moment on, the tension had been broken, just by an innocent comment, even if it did have obvious undertones in Bermondsey. The funeral took on a lighter tone that suited everybody. When Jon went back to the house at the end of the funeral, the family asked him to come in and have a cup of tea and a sandwich, which he happily did. One of the sisters, chatting to Jon, remarked, ''Ere, our brother, he was never very well; he was sick for years, you know. He had every operation you can imagine except for a hysterectomy.' Isn't that lovely? Typical Bermondsey, I tell you.

Jon left them after about fifteen minutes, with their brother put to rest and the family themselves feeling a little more relaxed than at the start of the day they had been dreading. I later received a lovely letter about Jon's conducting, a copy of which I keep to this day, as does Jon – both of us very proud!

Some of our staff too were born and bred in South London and grew up with that basic respect for the dead that I feel is commonplace in Bermondsey. Over the years, many characters have worked here, several of whom I have mentioned in my other books. One chap did part-time driving for us. When he started, we asked him if he had any problems dealing with dead bodies, and in particular how he would feel about having a dead body in the hearse

Never forget your roots. Living and working in the community in which I grew up has always filled me with pride.

Back in the 1960s – you can just see my legs on the far side of the coffin. Fred Albin leads a local funeral from just off Thorburn Square, Bermondsey.

In Bermondsey we often say goodbye in flowers.

An American metal casket is placed on the Rolls Hearse carried by the family and friends of the deceased.

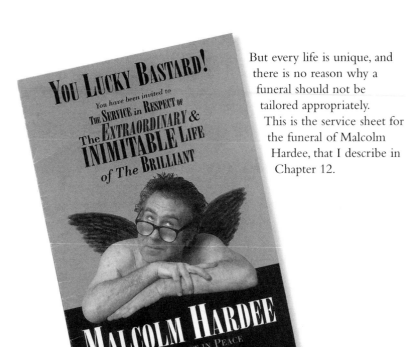

But every life is unique, and there is no reason why a funeral should not be tailored appropriately.

This is the service sheet for the funeral of Malcolm Hardee, that I describe in Chapter 12.

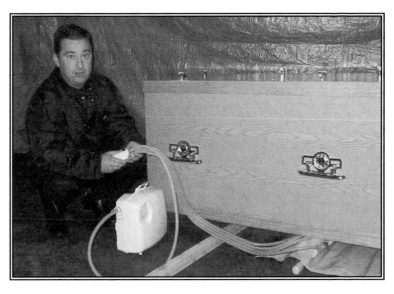

Dave operates the air-cushioned lifting system we use for some of the heavier people and coffins.

Another moment I will never forget as we all say goodbye to Lee. Lee's family will always be in my prayers. They are proud, excellent people.

One of the proudest and saddest moments in my career.
The Royal ceremonial for the ten members of the Armed Forces
killed when their Hercules aircraft crashed in Iraq.

Looking to the future. I know this great firm will be safe
in the hands of my sons, Simon and Jonathan.
But there's life in the old man yet!

behind him. 'Won't make any difference to me, mate,' he replied. 'I sleep with one every night anyway.' He isn't with the firm now, but I think I will keep his identity anonymous for the sake of his future wedded bliss.

Many people ring up asking for jobs here. One lady caller was particularly looking for a job in a mortuary. We suggested that she contact Guy's and St Thomas' mortuary and ask them about the possibility of a future job. We gave her the phone number but the next day she came in, having had no answer to her calls to the mortuary. 'You silly girl,' her mum had said, 'what do you expect? They're all bloody dead, ain't they, that's why you're getting no answer. You'd better go down to Albin's and get the directions and go there personally.' (I hate to disappoint you, Mum, but if they're dead and not answering the phone, they will hardly be likely to answer the door, will they?) We shared the joke with this lady, who eventually got a job in one of the mortuaries as hoped – she must have turned up on a day when the staff rather than the customers were answering the door.

People really do say the strangest things, don't they? I recently rang a crematorium and asked a new employee for the ashes of a particular person who had been cremated there. 'Do you have the ashes of Mr R. J. Jones available, please?' I asked her.

'Was he cremated?' she responded.

'Well, I hope so, love, otherwise I am wasting my time ringing you.'

'Sorry,' she said, seeing the funny side, 'of course he must have been. I've only been here a week and I'm still getting used to it. What a silly thing for me to say. Why else would you be ringing?'

This girl has now been at that crematorium office for several years and we often still joke about the incident. It is not a mistake she will make again, I promise you. We all do and say funny things without thinking clearly. But humour has to be at the centre of all things if there is to be some relief and some way forward.

Just the other day I was doing a radio interview about my campaign for funerals to use bus lanes (any support much appreciated, please!). It was a Saturday morning at about 7.30, and I was shaving. I mentioned to Jackie that I was going to receive a phone call because I was doing a radio interview. 'Oh,' she said, 'what time?'

'Eight o'clock,' I replied.

But when I turned round, there she was busily tidying everything up to make the bedroom look perfect. 'Jack, it's only an interview for the radio – it's not television; there's no one coming in here!'

She put her hand to her head and said, 'What am I doing? I just straight away thought I must get the place tidy.'

I don't know why she was bothering anyway as, to her credit, the place is never untidy.

Many years ago the business of funeral directing was very male-orientated. Over the last few decades, however, this has changed dramatically, and today there are many women working in all aspects of funeral directing. As with men, there are areas of funeral directing to which they are better suited. This is not a discriminatory comment but just common sense. Men and women all have different kinds of strengths and weaknesses.

One area in which I feel women are far superior to us men is in arranging funerals. Our lady funeral arrangers are, I like to say, the mums of the world. They do not have the monopoly on care, but I do believe that they have a head start. In general, they seem to be far easier to talk to than men and have a natural in-bred ability to listen, often relating more easily to a situation. They can put their arm around you with ease, and I think that speaking to a woman is definitely sometimes a little easier, so, girls, you have my vote on this one. In the conducting of funerals, however, I feel the contrary. My personal opinion is that men are stronger and better suited, although there will always be exceptions. I speak only generally, but you have to admit, ladies, that men do walk better in front of funerals. (Ouch, I'd better stop here before I get myself into trouble.)

The girls at Albin's are very hands-on and are prepared at any time to muck in with whatever has to be done or achieved. If a woman has died, it is often much more comforting for her family to know that she has been dressed by another woman and that her hair and make-up has been done by a woman, a policy that we have tried to adopt at Albin's. Likewise, we offer the same courtesy to men. On the rare occasion we have been asked for ladies to go and remove a deceased lady from her home, or when it has simply been a necessity because all the men are out employed on a funeral and the removal cannot wait, the girls just roll up their sleeves, lift up their skirts a little (so they can crouch down!) and get stuck in together as carefully and sensitively as they possibly can. We do, of course, have quality equipment, trolleys, lifting airbags and easy-moving equipment to make it possible. I have occasionally heard them comment with a little chuckle to themselves, 'You should have seen what you looked like when you pulled your skirt up to crouch down – what a sight!' but without a little humour how could you continue in such a job?

As long as you can always, for a moment, truly put yourself in the family's position, you will never forget how vital and important the work you do is. Being able to stand in another man's shoes for a moment, recognise that you are there and accept the situation is a true gift. My philosophy has not been, and never will be, that of the old-fashioned, elderly funeral director who said, 'Ay ay, boy, give 'em the bill whilst the tears are still in their eyes. Don't wait until they are past: you might never see the money.'

A number of years ago, one of our managers stopped, in our Volvo estate removal motor (with an empty stretcher in the back – clearly a funeral vehicle), at the chemist across the road to buy some cotton wool for the mortuary. Unfortunately, he left the key in the ignition as he thought he would only be a moment. When he came out, the inevitable had happened and the car had been stolen. We were, to say the least, shocked. The next morning when we arrived at work, we had the even greater shock of seeing, there outside in Culling Road, the stolen Volvo. Through the letterbox was the key, with a note: 'Sorry, we didn't know it belonged to you or we would never have taken it. Cheers!' Not right, of course, to have stolen it in the first place, but at least it shows that there is some honour among rogues and that Albin's is held in some esteem around this area. But you have to wonder, don't you, about the person who stole it – his train certainly didn't stop at all the stations.

Funny, isn't it, how you can sometimes reverse like this? Maybe initially fall out with somebody and then develop a mutual respect for one another, over the years remaining good companions. This happened to me many years ago at Grove Park Cemetery with a grave-digger called Sid, whom I am still friends with today. We were at the graveside during this particular funeral, and I was waiting for the priest to bless the grave so that I could lower the webs, which are provided by the cemetery to lower the coffin into the grave. There were about fifty people around the graveside, and standing on top of a stone at the back was Sid, who was new at the cemetery. He was making all kinds of signs and gestures, and, never having met him before, I thought him quite mad. Just as the minister finished blessing the coffin and as it rested gently at the bottom of the grave, in burst Sid. 'Can I have those straps back?' he cried.

'I think not,' I replied, and asked him to kindly stand back from the grave and wait patiently.

'But . . .' he uttered.

'But nothing, sir. Would you please wait quietly over to the left and I will be with you in good time? Now just please be patient.'

When the minister had finished blessing the congregation and the deceased, and we had all turned away from the grave, I took Sid by the arm over to a quiet area about fifty yards away and, in no uncertain manner put him straight about his behaviour. His point was that he wanted those straps for another interment that had arrived a little earlier than it should have done, but because he was unaware of the practice or of any form of dignity that had to be applied to his job (having come from working on the council), he just burst in and expected to get them back at a highly inappropriate moment. Unfortunately for him, he chose the wrong person to interrupt, and I lectured him for about five minutes on 'respect'.

Don't get me wrong: I have every consideration for the people who do this work. Grave-digging is a hard and sometimes thankless task – cold, wet, muddy, unpleasant, an all-round tough job – and whatever grave-diggers are paid, they deserve more. This is extremely unusual behaviour from a grave-digger, but Sid did not know the ropes. But he certainly knows now! Sid is the most respectful and kind person I have ever met at a cemetery, and he and I are now good pals. He still tells the story of how I put him right that day: 'A bit of respect didn't hurt anyone.' Respect goes both ways – wouldn't you agree?

Elaine, one of our funeral arrangers who also looks after our catering, always makes sure that there is, on our return from funerals she has catered for, a nice sandwich and cup of tea for us when we go back – respect on all sides here, too! She is a marvellous caterer, and her food is first class. I asked her whether she's going to buy a new product I've recently read about – black tomatoes called Kumatos, which apparently have a slightly different taste but are naturally sweet and juicy. They would be ideal for funeral teas! I'm not sure, though, whether I'd go as far as black jellied eels, seafood and pie and mash, which are the tops in South London for funeral catering.

Going back to the funny things people do, staff will always tell you about the amusing incidents that occur when the family decide to carry the coffin themselves – a very moving and honourable thing to do, but one open to mishap. When a family say that they would like to carry the coffin, we first gather the people who are going to do it to guide them in what to do. This could be any number from one up to eight people, possibly with more than one set of bearers to cover going into and out of church. One thing we do is try to measure everyone up properly so that they are of equivalent height. Then we try to get them to relax, stand straight and walk slowly in small steps, always starting with the left foot. We also teach them how to pivot slowly round if making a turn, rather than making great strides and crossing their feet.

Despite all this, I cannot estimate the number of times – undoubtedly hundreds – that a family approach the coffin to bring it from the hearse or lift it on to their shoulders, only to find that the person at the foot is facing forward but the person in the middle has turned completely the other way round, now facing the head of the coffin as well as the person behind. Now, which way will the coffin go if everyone is facing in different directions? More often than not, the person who is facing the wrong way, wherever they are in the bearing party, does not actually catch on to what has happened. When we point it out, they look as if to say, 'What a fool I have been,' but that is not the case – so often, it just reflects the nervousness of the situation and can actually help to relieve the tension.

Many of the funny stories concerning staff of course come from the younger members, the apprentices. As in all professions, they will be teased and have the occasional practical joke played on them. In an earlier chapter, I mentioned two of our current apprentices – baby-faced brothers Perry and Danny, or Winkle and Dinkle, Smash and Grab, as we call them. Winkle was the young man who appeared in the TV programme, the one who had all those attempts at his driving theory test. I have to tell you, though, that both he and Dinkle passed their practical driving tests first time.

I believe and hope that this is truly the profession for them, and they have already shown enormous signs of being dedicated to the job, but at the end of the day it must be remembered they are normal youngsters as well. We sometimes have to keep quite a tight rein on them, but they understand that. I sincerely hope that they fulfil their apprenticeships (time alone will tell). However, they still have a little way to go, as we will see.

Dinkle, who is quite quick-witted, was recently at a crematorium waiting to bear the coffin at one particular funeral. One of the Co-op funeral staff, an elderly man, said to him, 'What you doing here, son? You should be at school.'

Dinkle looked back at him. 'No, I shouldn't.'

'Yes, you should, you're nothing but a baby.'

'Well,' retorted Dinkle, 'I think that you should be retired. I'm just starting on my career so please leave me alone. I don't know you, and you don't know me. Let's keep it that way.' Typical Dinkle, returning his colleague's friendly banter. In the end, we have a great deal of respect for the profession and for the work we all do, as well as for all the supporting professionals – ministers, hire car drivers, organists, cemetery and crematorium staff – all marvellous.

My son Simon has quite a dry sense of humour, a bit like Ross in the TV comedy *Friends*, whereas my other son, Jonathan, has a more saucy sense of humour. Simon is ruthless around a bit of DIY. When he was organising the kitchen and office area, where we all meet in the mornings, he decided to remove some old wiring, unfortunately cutting an essential telephone line in the process. When I eventually got to the kitchen, I saw Simon holding the two ends of the phone line, one in each hand, like a crucifix, making a junction between them and telling me it was all right, he could stay like that until the telephone engineer got there. He looked at me so woefully that I just had to laugh. He knew that humour was the right tool to handle the situation, hoping I would respond the same way. But, boy, can he be ruthless with a paintbrush and a pair of scissors. He'll empty the place out and probably throw away the things you want most. With me for a dad, it's a good job he has a sense of humour.

I'd like to move next to a piece that was written by a lovely lady from Downham called Queenie Mortimer, which I have edited slightly. Apart from being personally interesting, it shows that the job can contain dangers for the staff. The extract comes from a booklet called *Downham Pride*, after its original youngsters, from which all the proceeds are donated to St Christopher's Hospice and Goldsmiths Community Association (both very worthy causes). In a couple of paragraphs, Queenie reflects on her knowledge of Albin's and describes the Albin funeral business arriving in Downham from Bermondsey:

The Albins are from Bermondsey where they still have their funeral parlour. They purchased a house in Old Bromley Road, number 132. Quite a few times when my mother used to take me out she would wait a while, and this was because the beautiful shiny black horses were being attached to the hearse, and although my mother loved horses she was also very scared of them. Just before World War II the Albins opened premises in Bromley Road. When Bromley Hill Cemetery was bombed Mr Albin and his sons had the task of clearing up the scattered remains of old and new corpses. Sadly through having rubbed a shoulder so badly, a leakage from one or part of one of the pieces penetrated this wound, from which he shortly died. Thankfully his sons were able to carry on the profession which their family had earlier begun in Bermondsey. It was often heard from the elderly folk, 'Oh yes, you go to Albin's: they show respect and dignity whilst the others can't get you to the cemetery fast enough.'

And finally, a little poem written by my aunt, Jean Menday, to support my campaign for funerals to be able to use bus lanes.

Bus Lane Ballad
(Dedicated to all who make and enforce bus lane rules)

> *What an ironic twist of fate*
> *If you were late at Heaven's gate*
> *And St Peter said you've been so slow*
> *You've been redirected down below.*
> *Now we wouldn't wish that on anyone*
> *But it might just be your dad or mum*
> *(. . . or possibly even YOU)*

STRONG SHOULDERS

Bus lanes are empty (as is the bus)
In off-peak times, so what's all the fuss?
Why don't you just alleviate curses
And allow free access to all the hearses?

7

CEREMONIAL FUNERALS

Ever since I was a young boy growing up above the shop at Albin's, I have dreamt of one day being responsible for a royal funeral (something I still dream of today). Imagine the honour, dignity and splendour of such an event. It would definitely be the pinnacle of any funeral director's career, wouldn't you say?

I have of course been involved in many splendid funerals, and funerals of those on the edge of royalty, for example those of the Duke of Argyle, several lords and ladies, the Queen Mother's butler, celebrities and individuals from all around the world, as you may have read in my previous books. I have in the past been privileged to make some royal coffins and have provided funerals for many church dignitaries, so it is fair to say that I have certainly had my moments and have come as close as is possible without actually achieving it to that crowning glory of royal funerals. Who knows, maybe this honour will still befall me or my sons. What I can be sure of, however, is that, for the funeral directors entrusted with such an honour, it is a higher responsibility.

In the past year, because of our involvement with the Ministry of Defence and the repatriation of soldiers who have been killed abroad, I have been very honoured to have been involved in many ceremonial funerals. The planning of ceremonial funerals, as with royal funerals, is very complex and complete. You practise until you drop. Everything is timed to the minute – in fact, to the second. No stone is left unturned, and there are no surprises. The most meticulous detail must be attended to, and there must be no mistakes. The preparation is exhausting but the end result rewarding, and I have been fortunate enough to meet some incredible people from the military who have great experience of preparing ceremonial funerals. I have certainly enjoyed the experience of working with them, and I hope the feeling is mutual.

How can I tell you all about these complex, pre-arranged ceremonial funerals without boring you with detail? I think the best way is for me to tell you about when I first met Tom, who is probably the top man in ceremonial military funerals. Let me first describe him to you. Tom is the epitome of sartorial elegance, everything you would expect from a Garrison Sergeant Major. Upright, smart, focused, fearsome yet with a kind streak in him, passionate, understanding, not a man to cross and, believe me, totally in charge.

The first ceremonial service I completed was for two soldiers who had been killed in action in Iraq (*Bury My Heart in Bermondsey* tells the story), and it was my responsibility to bring them home. We were put on alert and instructed that we must be at Brize Norton airbase in Oxfordshire on the day before their return. We had to take two hearses (one for each soldier), a full accompaniment of staff and a third hearse as a reserve in case one hearse broke down at the start of the ceremony. There were to be two practice coffins, of correct size and weight for each of the soldiers, which had to be estimated from reports we were given by Simon and Christopher, of our sister company Kenyon Christopher Henley, and a further one with no added weight at all. Added to this were to be two sets of trestles and of course Albin's/Kenyon Christopher Henley 'ceremonial dress' (also the epitome of sartorial elegance).

We were to report at 7.30 a.m. on the day before the soldiers were to return. We signed in, collected our passes and were met by a Squadron Leader who has since become a very good friend of mine.

'Righto chaps,' he said. 'Who's in charge? Step forward.'

'I am. I'm Barry Albin-Dyer.'

He extended his hand and said, 'Barry himself! I have heard so much about you, it's lovely to meet you.'

'Really?' I said.

'Of course. I've read your first book. You are a legend.' (They were his words not mine, I assure you, and they became the start of a strong friendship!)

We were next introduced to the base Commander, who formally welcomed us and thanked us for being prompt and organised. Then we met the Warrant Officer who was responsible for the RAF's part in this ceremonial funeral. He spent an hour or so just walking me through the preliminaries of the ceremony, for which I was very grateful.

Basically, these were as follows. By 7.30 the next morning we were to be in position by the side of the arrival lounge, out of sight, in full formal dress with both hearses, funeral directors and the reserve hearse in place, started and running. At precisely 7.58 a.m., a C17 plane would arrive from Iraq with red, white and blue blasting from the back to honour the dead. The C17 would touch down on the runway at precisely 8.00 a.m. – to the second. It would taxi round and deflare itself, the flares being necessary for diverting missiles should it be attacked as it left Iraq. It would taxi round at exactly 8.10 a.m. and stop on a precisely marked area outside the terminal.

While this was happening, the top brass would, at exactly 7.55, be walking out with the family of the deceased and would stand about fifty yards from the plane's eventual destination. As the C17 stopped, its back doors would drop and I would be given my nod to proceed. I would then page the funeral around (that is, walk in front of it) and park directly opposite on a precise spot pointed out to me by the Warrant Officer on the ground outside the terminal. During this, I was to pause and tip my hat to the dignitaries and the family as a mark of respect. I would stop at a precise point, remove my hat, walk around to the driver's door, pass my hat and stick and gloves to the driver, walk to the back of the hearse, open the back door, slide out the bier so that it protruded just past the rear of the hearse, remove the stops and stand straight, perfectly in line with the side door of the plane.

While this was going on, Tom, the Garrison Sergeant Major, and his team of bearers, all friends from the same regiment as the deceased soldiers, would march smartly in line out to the aircraft and already be in place alongside the coffins inside the C17. When, through the plane window, they saw me stand perfectly still by the side of the hearse, they would begin, slowly and with great dignity, to carry their departed friends from the aircraft, one at a time. They would march across the airfield towards the dignitaries and the hearse, and stop at a precise point for one second as the bugler played the Last Post. At this point, the bearers would turn, slow walk towards the hearse, stand and turn sideways to the coffin, bring it from their shoulders gently down into their hands and then side-foot close to the bier, where they would, ceremonially and in line, shuffle the coffin into the back of the hearse. I was to encourage them quietly as they did so.

When this procedure had been completed, they would side-foot back and stand perfectly still while I walked to the head of the coffin, pushed in the bier, entered the stop and closed the back. I would then bow, walk across, get into the hearse and slowly taxi around the C17, across the airport and round to the chapel of rest. This procedure would be repeated by the second hearse, and we would arrive together at the chapel. The coffins would be laid out in the chapels, and after about fifteen minutes, the families would be brought along, one at a time.

This point, when the family leave the vehicle, is very important as they are introduced to me for the first time. From then on in such a ceremony, I am totally responsible for that family – for any questions they may ask, for showing them in to be with their son or daughter, for caring for them. When we leave the chapel and walk back to the vehicle that will then take them home, the responsibility passes back to the member of the military who has been looking after them since the death.

There were very definite boundaries of responsibility involved. A family in those circumstances are often angry or need to blame somebody, or maybe they are distraught. The first thing that I try to do is greet them with a pleasant smile, a warm handshake and sincere affection, which I hope they can feel emanate from me. I am not there to defend the undefendable. I am not there to put anything right that has gone wrong before this point. I cannot answer for the death of their son or daughter or the rights and wrongs of war. I can only say to them that, from this point on, I will answer all their questions truthfully. I will see that they have everything they want, all the knowledge they need and all the comfort I can possibly give.

There are many things they may want to know. What

happens next? When can we see our son/daughter? When do we get a death certificate? Will we be able to look at our son/daughter rather than just sit with them in the chapel quietly for a few moments with a closed coffin? How will the funeral be arranged? Who will be conducting the funeral? Who will pay for the funeral? How long will it all take? Many of the potentially endless questions can be answered by the Coroner's Officer, some by me, but they must all be dealt with. I think it is very professional of the Ministry of Defence to have a funeral director there to do this, and I have found the Ministry to be very supportive of my work. The family and I might spend an hour together so that they fully understand what is going on and all their questions have been answered.

At this point, the family is taken home by the Ministry of Defence and we transport the son or daughter to the Coroner's Office at the John Radcliffe Hospital in Oxford, where a small investigation will begin. After about twenty-four hours, we return to the John Radcliffe Hospital, collect the deceased and bring them to Bermondsey. They are then prepared for their final journey home, which could be to anywhere in the British Isles, or indeed the world. We will take them wherever their family home is or wherever their family wishes, where the funeral will take place, often with a family funeral director whom they may have known for years and they have chosen themselves. If the family does not have a funeral director, we may be able to continue the work and undertake the funeral.

Those few hours with the family are the most difficult hours I ever spend as a funeral director or bereavement counsellor. And if it is demanding for me, how must it be for that family? That thought constantly sustains me. I am still in touch with one or two of the families, which is really nice. Trust is everything, and if you can gain people's trust and show them patience, dignity, respect – above all, if you can listen – it will come right in the end. I cannot bring their loved one back, but I can be there.

But back to my first practice and preparation for the events I have described above. After my first hour or so with the Warrant Officer, I was taken over to an aircraft hangar. I was amazed at what I saw there. In the corner was a complete replica of the inside of a C17, and alongside it a replica of a Chinook helicopter. These are where the military can practise loading these aircraft so that they can be balanced properly and so that personnel can work out exactly how much they can get on each plane when it arrives or departs. Today, this was to practise carrying the coffins to and from the hearse, something that we, as a team, did endless times that day.

This was where I first met Tom, a striking figure to say the least. We drove the hearse in and stood quietly by the back of it. Tom kept looking at me, which made me feel slightly uncomfortable for a moment. Eventually he marched smartly over to me and said, 'How do you do? My name is Tom. You are . . . ?'

'My name is Barry. How do you do, sir?'

'No,' said Tom, 'that is your first mistake. My name is Tom. How do you do, Barry?'

Again I said, 'How do you do, Tom? Nice to meet you, sir.'

'No, my name is Tom,' he repeated.

It was so hard to call him Tom: because of the way he was dressed and the fact that his persona oozed the request to be called sir. I am sure you know what I mean.

'Have I met you before, sir?' he said to me.

'First mistake, Tom,' I said. 'My name is Barry.'

'Very good, Barry,' he said.

'No, I haven't met you before, Tom.'

'Are you sure?' he said. 'Your face is very familiar to me. Have you been on any of my royal funerals or other ceremonies?'

'No, I haven't, sir – oops, Tom,' I replied.

'Ahh, interesting. Anyway it will come to me,' he said. 'I will be with you in a moment.' And off he marched to the lads.

The men who were going to carry the coffin were all very young, probably not much older than nineteen, and were, quite rightly, terribly unnerved by the whole event. The trestles and coffins were removed from the back of the aircraft, and Tom spent some time with the lads on the aircraft practising lifting: up, down, up, down. This is why he had needed a loaded coffin – to get the balance right and to check that the lads could cope with the weight. He had asked for an unloaded coffin because practising time and time again with a weighted coffin would have exhausted them.

About half an hour passed before Tom's head peered round the back of the C17 across the hangar. He marched smartly over to me and held out his hand: 'You're the man. Mr Don't Drop the Coffin, that's you. My wife loves you. She's watched the whole programme. Wait till I tell her I've met you.'

'Thank you, Tom,' I replied.

'That's it; I knew I'd get you. Lovely to meet you. I'll be with you again in a moment,' and off he went. What a character, fantastic!

Next began our part of the practice, and Tom told me in detail the procedure I described above. Time and time again, the lads carried the coffin to the back of the hearse, but they could not get it successfully on to the centre of the bier – it was all one side or the other. At this point the temptation to interfere was overwhelming and at last I opened my mouth.

'Excuse me, sir.'

'My name is Tom,' came the stark reply, 'remember, *Tom!*'

'Tom, yes, I beg your pardon. Can I be of assistance to you here? If I mark the hearse with two pieces of tape either side and the boys put the edge of the foot of the coffin on each piece of tape, the coffin can begin its journey on to the bier completely straight. I will put two wider pieces of tape at the shoulder area so that the men at the shoulder will see, as it reaches the tape, whether it's one side or the other and they can move it gently over.'

On the first attempt, this system worked perfectly. Tom, excited by the success, stood back.

'There we are. There we are, boys. That's why this man is here – because he is a bleeding expert, that's why, a bleeding expert. Thank you very much, Barry.'

Everybody smiled, and we carried on practising. After about another hour or so of up, down, in, out, off we went to the main airfield for hours of dress rehearsal, something I had not expected at all. I thought we would end our practice in the hangar, but no, Tom wanted a full dress rehearsal. So there we were, on the runway with an actual C17 in place, cold, windblown and, unbeknown to me, still with another four or five hours of practice in front of us. As we arrived at the area of runway outside the departure and arrival lounges, Tom walked over with all the lads and said, 'Now, lads, we are going to have a proper dress rehearsal here. This gentleman has already assisted us, and he is Mr Don't Drop the Coffin, and what won't we do tomorrow? That's right, we won't drop the coffin. These are your buddies coming back here tomorrow, and we're going to do them proud, lads. Now Barry, let me walk you through what you are going to do tomorrow.'

'I'll just stop you there for a moment, Tom. I've already been walked through by the Warrant Officer. I know exactly where my spot is and what I am to do.'

'Excuse me, Barry; have I walked you through this?'

'No, Tom, I did it this morning . . .'

'If I haven't walked you through, then you haven't done it.'

And Tom began to tell me exactly how I would do everything with the hearse just round the side as I described and at his particular nod. At this point, he walked across to the back of the C17 and stood still. 'Barry –' and he pointed at himself clearly from the top of his head – 'watch!' and he nodded his head. 'That is my key, and that is my time to walk off.' He marched smartly over and asked, 'Did you see me? Did you see my head move? That is your command.'

'Thank you, Tom, I've got it,' I replied. He left me in no doubt, and quite right too. As I have said before, it's all 'preparation, preparation, preparation'.

'At this point, you will walk round at a good pace, please: not too slow and not too fast,' he continued.

As we walked along, I came to a painted spot on the floor where I was to stop. 'This is my spot, Tom. I am stopping on it.'

He looked at the spot. Then he looked across at the building parallel with the spot and said, 'That is no longer your spot.'

'Oh no,' I thought, 'I knew exactly my spot and now it's about to change.'

'Your spot now is the stanchion across at the side of the building.'

'Very good, Tom, but that's in line with the spot so it's the same place.'

'Good point, Barry, but tomorrow that stanchion will be

there, and knowing the RAF (with no disrespect) that spot might not be. The stanchion is your stopping spot.'

'Fair enough, Tom,' I said, and off we went again, practising every last detail, no stone left unturned.

An Army captain walked out of the terminal and asked me to cover up the hearse's number plate – AlBIN – as the letter 'l' looked like a number 1, making A1-BIN, which he did not feel was appropriate. I advised him it stood for Albin, our name, and not any type of bin, but it was easier to put some tape over the l, which satisfied him. First thing next morning, while waiting for the C17 to land, the camp police officer warned me to remove the tape. I explained why it was there, but he replied, with no sympathy for my plight, 'I don't care. Remove it before you leave the base or I'll nick you.' What a nice man. Sometimes you just can't win.

By now, the lads were a bit tired so Tom took us all round the back of the hangar for a cup of tea. One particular lad, who can only have been about seventeen, was very nervous and having trouble getting his footwork in line with the others'. It was wearing Tom out, but not as much as it was fatiguing this poor lad. Quietly and off the record, I offered him a few gentle words of advice to try and straighten him up a bit. Tom then brought the coffin into the hangar at the side of the departure lounge where we were having our tea to give the lad a private lesson. But the lad got it wrong again on the first move.

'Put the coffin down; put it down now,' ordered Tom.

Then Tom grabbed the lad at the back of the shoulders and marched him out, away from everybody, to the back of the warehouse. We heard such a bang, crash, wallop, ouch, ohh . . . and everyone was wondering what was going on. Seconds later, Tom walked back with the lad, who was rubbing his head and holding his arm. 'I warned you, lad,' he said, 'now get it right or else.' Everybody was looking very shocked when, all of a sudden, the lad burst out laughing and so did Tom. It was a complete farce, and nothing had happened at all. It was just a spoof to break the ice and take the tension off the moment. Funnily enough, the lad got it all perfect on his next drill. Tom just knew that it had become too serious at that point and he needed to do something.

Back we went to the runway for another rehearsal. The poor bugler had been standing outside for several hours; his lips were cold and he couldn't get any spit at all. We reached the point at which the bugler was to play – but there was *nothing*. Tom's head appeared around the coffin. 'Stop! Son, are you going to play or are we standing here until tomorrow?' at which point Tom ordered us back to the beginning and we started again. This time the bugler did begin to play but he soon blew a wrong note. 'Stop! See you, boy, you've got lips like Mick Jagger. Get in there and warm them up.'

At this point, Tom felt it necessary to walk over to me and say, 'Barry, if I don't use a little humour with the lad it will break him, and that will be no good for him, me or anybody. It's not that I don't think this is a serious matter – you do understand that, don't you?' He was concerned that I thought he was mocking or being too light-hearted. On the contrary, he was brilliant.

We finished our rehearsal, and Tom felt that he had things right. I was confident that I knew everything would be OK. I was now to have a meeting with the Squadron Leader to run through the family names and find out whom I was meeting and exactly what was required. We cleaned the hearses, put them into an aircraft hangar for the night and went off to a local hotel to have a bath, change and get something to eat. I spent several hours going through in my mind exactly what would happen the next day– who was I meeting? what were the names? – so that I got it right.

The next morning we arrived at the base bright and early. The whole atmosphere had changed. We were met by the military police and the Squadron Leader, and were taken to the precise area where we had rehearsed the day before. There we were: 7.30 a.m., three hearses, the staff dressed immaculately, photographers, press, top brass, everything ready. Precisely to the second, the C17 arrived and went through the routine expected of it. Everything was perfect to the last step. I reached my spot – no, I'm sorry, my stanchion – at exactly the right time. The boy who had trouble carrying the day before carried immaculately. The spirit of the lads, tears in their eyes, was moving and emotional. The drained expressions of the family did not mask their pride, and possibly a little bit of suppressed anger.

I spent a great deal of time with the families that day. They were lovely people, faces that I will never forget. I guess that moment changed me for ever. Sure, I was finally doing ceremonial funerals, and as a funeral director I was very proud to be involved in them, but as a person I was drained with emotion. Everything went perfectly – completely perfectly. The next week I received a letter from Tom to say thanks and send an invitation to his mess for dinner one afternoon. I sent back a copy of my book, signed for his wife, and a reply saying how much meeting him had changed my life and what a privilege it had been.

I really do feel well and truly prepared and ready for whatever lies in front of me at any future ceremonial funeral. I thought at that point that I had seen more or less all that could be seen, experienced more or less all that could be experienced in such an event. What I had never imagined was that, only a few months down the line, we would be going off to Iraq to collect a seventeen-year-old local boy by the name of Lee O'Callaghan, whose tale, with his family's permission, I will disclose to you now.

A local lad from Walworth, Lee was known to all of us at Albin's, as were his lovely family, whom I admire and respect beyond words. Only a few months earlier, we had had a funeral for Lee's family and were chatting to him about the possibility of his possibly going to Iraq in the coming months. I never dreamt then that it would be the last time I would ever see him alive. The day that Lee was killed trying to save his pals and commanding officer, his aunty came directly into the office, knowing that I would be involved in bringing Lee back. To her and to Lee's mum and dad, Shirley and Eugene, this was a wonderful comfort.

From then on, all of us at Albin's just wanted to get there and get Lee home. Two of my lads went out there immediately, while I prepared for the ceremonial service and greeting of Lee as he came home. All the preparations for the ceremonial funeral were made and carried out as I had done before, but on this occasion I was at the airport much earlier. The Ministry of Defence had asked me to greet the family, as I knew them so well, and to introduce them to the commanding officers. Lee's parents, brother and sister, aunties, all the family were there. We shared a very emotional greeting. Lee, of course, came back here to Bermondsey with us, and for the first time I saw the continuing side of a ceremonial funeral. We sat down with Lee's family, his commanding officers, police commanders, priests, everybody who would be involved on the day of the funeral, and planned the route, the preparation, the ceremony, everything down to the smallest detail yet again.

Lee was to have a military funeral with all military honours – a wonderful tribute to his family. Lee had wanted to be a soldier all his life. His lifetime ambition had been to join his regiment – the First Battalion the Princess of Wales Royal Regiment – and he was prepared to go to Iraq and do his duty. Lee had phoned his parents a few days before his death, telling them that the first part of his tour of duty had gone very well but that it was now getting quite scary out there. He said he was looking forward to coming home in about three weeks' time, but little did he or anyone else know how he would be coming home.

The funeral was a great tribute to Lee and his family, a magnificent affair with over twenty limousines, several hearses for flowers and many of his friends flown in from Iraq. Soldiers from his regiment and pals were to carry his coffin. His family priest gave a wonderful tribute to his life. There were readings from his aunties and commanding officers, with doves released at the graveside and a firing party providing a last salute. Buglers, music and a trip through the football ground at Millwall, where his beloved team paid great honour to him on the Saturday after he died by bringing his family on to the pitch for a minute's silence. It was a funeral I will never forget. Perhaps my first full ceremonial funeral, start to finish.

Only a week later, another young man, this time from Lewisham in South London, was killed. Although Albin's did not complete his final interment, last Christmas we held a special tribute at our annual Memorial Service in our Garden of Rest, a tribute to every soldier lost in this particular conflict. We invited Lee's family and the family of the other young soldier who had died, and paid a special tribute by reading the names of every soldier who had been lost. The military were involved, the flag was raised and lowered, the Last Post played and doves released in their memory. It was a wonderful evening and I will never forget the emotion of those two families, embracing as if they had known each other their whole lives, bonded by the loss of their sons, both heroes but both lost to this world. May they find true peace in the next.

And I wish the same to every person who has lost their life in conflict throughout history. For all of them, it should not have been their time.

8

TRADITIONS, CUSTOMS
AND THE LINGO

If there is a spokesperson for the Natural Death Centre, which of course there is, why isn't there one for the 'unnatural death centre' (not that one exists)? Obviously, not everything has an opposite, and as a funeral director I am well aware that one should not assume anything. But one can probably safely assume that many of the words in the dictionary can be abbreviated, lengthened or adapted to suit any situation, including the language of death.

Historically, the lingo of death often has its origins in other languages. Sometimes this language is startling, occasionally obvious, never dull, and from time to time very colourful, especially in cockney! One local character recently told me exactly the kind of memorial he wants when he is dead: 'Bal, when I die I want you to take an impression of my arse. Then I want you to have it bronzed and put on top of my grave with a little hole at the vital spot where anyone who cares can put flowers, anyone who don't like me can kick it, anyone who don't care can just kiss my arse, and anyone who don't know me can park their bike there. I don't give a monkey's.' Humorous, of course, but I'm not so sure he was joking, I'm really not. They often remark that it's the language we use that makes life interesting and helps to define us, even if occasionally such language is unpleasant.

I received an e-mail from Squadron Leader Rob Rowntree who had read my last book *Bury My Heart in Bermondsey*, which he said he had enjoyed very much. He offered me a sort of alternative 'RAF speak', as he called it, to my cockney banter. So here are a few translations, cockney first, then RAF speak (posh banter):

- Oi oi saveloy, Bal me old china / I say, old chap.
- 'Ere for you to have a butcher's hook at / For your perusal.
- Mate, that looks the dogs / Top notch, old chap.
- Me old trouble and strife / The Mem Sahib.
- Hold up, 'ave a look / Bandits at one o'clock.
- Cor, mate, who dropped that? / Chocks away, that's hit the spot.
- Who cares, park it anywhere / Tits up, on the pan, Dunlops down.
- Cheers, me old pal, 'ere we go / Tally ho.
- Wait on, pal, you're the governor, Bal / Stand by one, top man, Bazza.

If I'd learnt the lingo, I might have done quite well in the RAF, you never know. But I think I may have been even better off in the WRAF; that *would* have been nice!

When we in South London have an occasional run in with what we might describe as 'a snob', the language can be quite interesting in itself. Lee recently had an altercation with such a lady; she was riding a bicycle while Lee was driving a limousine on his way back from a funeral. The lady had decided, quite incorrectly, that she had right of way on this bike and that the world should stop for her. Lee simply remarked to her, 'Lady, you shouldn't be riding there.'

She replied, 'How dare you speak to me in such a way, young man. Who do you think you are? I am riding my bike here.'

But Lee retorted, 'Lady, what a snotty person you are, and bloody inconsiderate. Can't you think of other people?'

She screamed out at him, obviously offended by the word 'snotty': 'I'm not snotty. Hey, you there, chauffeur, I'm not snotty.'

Lee quite rightly took no further notice and went about his journey, the lady still demonstrating, 'I'm not snotty.'

Sorry, madam, that's exactly what you are!

Anybody who knows our mechanic Kenny or has read descriptions of him in my previous books will remember that Kenny speaks two languages – South London cockney and profanity – each with equal ease. On the way back from one funeral, I suffered the misfortune, which rarely happens, that the hearse had failed to continue (not broken down, simply failed to continue). Kenny, in his breakdown van, set out to find me and the hearse. He was having some difficulty, and while sitting at a set of traffic lights in Kensington was looking at his little A–Z map to see how close he was to the right turn he needed. Unfortunately, it seems that Kenny's indicator had not corrected itself at the previous traffic lights and was still flashing as if to turn right. As Kenny was looking at his map, there was a tap on his window. Yes, you've guessed it, another snotty lady on a push bike. Kenny rolled down the window. This time, she had picked on the wrong person as, quite frankly, Kenny could not give a damn (or a f**k in his language).

'You, driver,' she cried, 'do you know that you are misleading the traffic?'

'What, lady?' he said.

'You're misleading the traffic,' she repeated.

'What are you talking about, you silly cow?' said he. 'Mind your own business.'

'How dare you speak to me in such a fashion?' she replied.

'Go away, lady, or you'll get a lot worse,' retorted Kenny, at which point she should have taken the hint and gone on her way. But no, she persisted, at which point Kenny rolled up his newspaper, put his arm out of the window and tapped her across the top of the head with the paper, hitting the bobble on her hat. Not a good thing to do, I know, and I certainly do not advocate this kind of violence at any point, but it was a harmless flick of a piece of paper on top of her head, and it did have the effect of stopping her in her tracks and bringing her down to earth again. 'I told you, lady, mind your own business,' and he drove off up the road.

Kenny should not, of course, have done that, but she *was* dicing with death. She really had met someone who was her match, someone who couldn't give a monkey's. When I heard what had happened, I told Kenny not to behave in such a fashion again, but I somehow don't think it's sunk in. You have to laugh, though, haven't you? If you didn't, you'd cry.

But away from Kenny's lingo, and back to the lingo of death. The discovery of death must have been quite a shock to early man. If you stop and think about it, the fact that we know that death exists gives value to life itself, and losses become expected even if not often accepted. This leads us to our rituals related to the process of parting with someone we have lost and the language we eventually use to describe that process, which we could even describe as a language of the dead. The process of burying our dead goes back a very long way – modern archaeologists have discovered through the excavation of graves and the study of burial rituals that it goes as far back as 120,000 years before Christ, too long even to be able to imagine. Since time immemorial, then, people have buried or cremated their dead, so if funeral customs are as old as civilisation itself, the funeral service clearly plays a part in the history of humankind, setting off the archaeological trails of funeral practice.

It is not unreasonable to assume that early man would

have been terrified of death and completely without any form of understanding of it. It is therefore also reasonable to assume that the taboo of death began with the very first witnessed death. We are all afraid of things we do not understand. In the very beginning, the dead would have been burnt, buried or just left to rot or be devoured by wild animals. So how far have we really come in understanding death? Have we actually made any progress at all? Death will always be the final mystery, the ultimate taboo, the stigma of life, and we carry the fear from just knowing that one day we all will have to face it: even my good friends from the Cryonics Institute are, at best, only extending life. Man will never live for ever in a physical sense, but I do believe that the soul goes on and on and that this is the sacred link between this world and the next.

Throughout my writings, I have often referred to funeral customs and superstitions, but what of the language of funerals? What is the origin of some of the words we use? Some origins have of course been lost in antiquity. Others still have a clear meaning today, and some are steeped in superstition and shrouded in mystery. So let's try to explain a few of the well-known commonly used words and phrases relating to the dead.

Funeral

This comes from the Latin *funeralis*, relating to the disposal of the dead from Roman times. The word also had something to do with torches in Roman times, when many funerals took place at night and needed torches to light the way (more custom than superstition).

Undertaker

In early days, this term was always used in its general sense: a person who undertook to do something that other people did not want to do or could not do. This developed in more modern terms to mean the provider of a funeral, particularly funeral furnishings and other such functions. It is believed that the first advert concerning an undertaker was published in New York in 1768. Since then, people have found all kinds of titles for somebody in my profession: funeral director, our modern term; mortician, as one would be known in the USA; thanatologist, more commonly known as embalmer; counsellor, grief therapist. I recently heard the American term 'celestial tour operator' (tickets, please!) and even 'man in black'. But by any other name, we are the same people.

Hearse

This is thought to come from the French word *herse*, meaning a harrow – not 'Harrow, how are you?' as the Chinese joke goes, but a triangular implement with spikes attached, originally used in the fields for breaking up soil but later adapted for candlesticks used in the ceremonial rights of the dead. These 'candlesticks', for want of a better word, were suspended over the tomb and later became converted into a vehicle like a wheeled bier to bear the casket from the home to the grave; this in turn was later converted to a carriage. Our modern funeral cars and hearses all originate from the old hearse, the pall and the bier, which houses the coffin. My dad would tell you, and I think he was right, that the first hearse was created along with the wheel, and I am sure that he would object to the idea of a relatively modern French origin – sorry, Dad!

Coffin

This too is from the Latin – *cophinus* – although it in turn comes from the Greek word *kophinos*, meaning a basket. Many, many years ago, wicker baskets were used by funeral directors to transport deceased people from their place of death to the mortuary. People often ask me the difference between a coffin and a casket. Well, a coffin is shaped at the shoulders to match the deceased, whereas a casket is oblong like the shape of a door. Simple.

Cemetery

From the Greek (again) *koimeterion*, meaning a dormitory or sleeping place, so even then the association between death and sleeping existed.

Pall

The *pallium* was a cloak or cover held by a Roman pall-bearer, who would hold the pall aloft on a pole like a kind of canopy, providing protection for the coffin and the coffin-bearers. At Sir Winston Churchill's funeral, there were, preceding the coffin from the church, dignitaries who were referred to as 'pall-bearers'. The coffin was carried by soldiers, who were the 'bearers'.

Autopsy

(Probably Latin.) Literal interpretation 'to see with one's own eyes' (that's my favourite) – perfect!

Mausoleum

This again hails from Greece. In about 370 BC, Mausolus, the king of Caria, designed his own huge marble tomb in which his body was to be housed after death. The word is now used for a place that commemoratively houses the dead.

Here, however, are a couple of terms that you will not recognise as being associated with the dead.

Dole

The Latin *dolere* means simply 'to grieve'. Many years ago, mourning clothes called 'doole' (derived from the Latin) were distributed to the poor. Hence 'doole' became something given away in relation to death itself and bereavement. Today, of course, it refers to signing on and receiving state benefits.

Deadbeat

Years ago, if you wanted to travel around England, you had to pass through toll gates. Crossing a piece of land would earn a toll, a payment, but corpses were given free passage. In effect, they were beating the toll, hence the term 'deadbeat'. The term now really relates to people who shirk their responsibilities or have no real use in life (not a term I could condone because truly everybody has a use in life).

Lich-gate (or lych-gate)

And here's a word deriving not from Latin or Greek, but from the German word *Leiche*, meaning a corpse. This was the gate at the front of the church where the coffin was placed on two small supports upon the gate while waiting for the congregation and family to assemble before processing into the churchyard and the church.

So there you are, Latin, French, Greek and German origins. Perhaps we can claim one British (probably Irish, as this was to begin with an Irish tradition) origin, though – for the 'wake', which means the watching over the corpse. In the past, people would sit with the corpse and watch over it. Others would often have to travel far for a funeral and might arrive at any time during the night before the funeral, then being offered refreshments, as they are still today. So the wake became a pre-funeral celebration. Today in the UK, we of course have the wake at the end of the funeral – and very splendid affairs they often are too, in Bermondsey anyway.

There always has been, and always will be, funeral lingo. When my sons reach my age, their funeral lingo may be extended to funeral Internet lingo. Perhaps funerals will be broadcast on the net so that those who are unable to attend from thousands of miles away may also take part in some way in that day's experience. There will probably be electronic guest books, with everything transferred on to DVD for people to keep. Who can tell? I hope I am still around to hear the lingo that emerges from that technology.

Funeral language is already turning trendy in its use of abbreviations and jargon. Like every industry, funeral directors use personalised terminology between themselves and connected professions. Remember the terms (mentioned in one of my previous books) that are used for international repatriation on aircraft – 'horizontal passengers' and 'HMs' (human remains)? Well, I will let you into a little secret and tell you a few of these jargon terms now:

- the dead house – the funeral home (Irish, that one);
- the morgue – the mortuary;
- the box – the coffin;
- Tom mix – five feet six inches: the size of the person;
- a single-seater – a hearse;
- a lim – a limousine;
- to pivot – to turn with the coffin;
- to bear – to carry a coffin;
- to bury – to inter a deceased;
- a crem – a crematorium;
- a cem – a cemetery;
- a home take – resting somebody at home;
- a church take – resting somebody in church overnight;
- a removal – removing somebody from a home, nursing home, mortuary or hospital;
- the twelve o'clock – funerals are often referred to by their time, such as 'the four o'clock';
- to coffin up – to place somebody in the coffin, their final place of rest;
- the road map – the chapel list;
- a hearse and one – a hearse and one following limousine.

Wherever there is a term or a word, people will in some way shorten it or come up with a slang version. We even refer to the music at funerals as the 'funeral hit parade', with such famous hits as 'My Way', 'The Wind Beneath My Wings', 'Ave Maria', 'Time to Say Goodbye', 'Dance with My Father Again', 'The Living Years' and 'Somewhere Over the Rainbow'. A funeral director has to have these at hand. We have literally hundreds and hundreds of recordings for people to choose from. In time, I guess that this will be superseded by the Internet: you can download almost anything, at a price, if you put your mind to it. You can have all the technology in the world, but there eventually has to be a 'doer'. I like to think of us all here as doers, and the more doers we have, the better kind of world we will achieve – that's my philosophy, anyway.

I would like to end this chapter with a poem that was written by a brilliant sixteen-year-old Iranian girl, living in America with her family, only days before her own sudden and unexpected death from a massive asthma attack. Did she have some kind of premonition? This shows how language can be used to express such wonderful purpose and meaning, as well as fear. This piece leaves me for ever in deep thought and melancholy. What a loss to the world. Surely everything this young girl was to her family and to this world cannot end here?

Immortality

In dreams I have had my family has cried
Why her? Why strike youth?
Why do you take our souls and hearts and minds?

and in these dreams I stand there confused
at my funeral and the dirges played
and I want to cry out to them
Yet I am alive!

Nothing so cowardly as death can overcome me
can surmount my persisting youth.
For my soul is here within me
and cannot be removed by such fumbling hands as death's.

And then I wake and am surrounded
by vicious reminders of my weakness
for I will die just as everyone before me.
Don't I deserve better for myself?

So in my waking hours I become the me of my dreams
and my dreams no longer comfort
but terrify.

So Why? Why not immortality?

9

WHAT IS THIS ILLNESS WE CALL BEREAVEMENT?

As I sit in my office writing, I casually glance at my clock. It is ten o'clock on Saturday 12 February 2005. But why have I just looked at the date and time? We live, we die, and ultimately none of these details means anything. Yet in this fragile world everything means something. If one philosophy definitely applies to life, does the opposite philosophy also apply? For example, even if we are a twin, we are, at the moment of birth, alone; yet it does not follow that we have to die alone. But then, are we ultimately alone at the moment of our last breath? It seems that it is death's journey that we are really afraid of – the unknown, the ultimate journey, the mystery of death itself.

In the first chapter, I talked about how a funeral director's care is similar to that of a parent who is rocking the cradle of a child perhaps in pain from teething or colic, comforting it to sleep. Never is this type of responsibility needed more than after a funeral, when one is really alone, often bewildered, empty and numb. It is then that our cradle must be rocked and our pain eased. This pain can be eased, and enough strength and courage can be found to live the life we have left to us, and this we must do and can do, with help.

I was eager to get all these rushing thoughts on to paper, but at that very moment the phone rang. When a funeral director's phone rings, it is obviously rarely good news for somebody, and I certainly do not sit at my desk eagerly waiting for the phone to ring to increase my business. But I am always here to rock the cradle when it is needed, and my profession is more than a business or a money-making venture: it is my very existence. On answering the phone, I was confronted with the immediate personal pain of bereavement and the shock that it brings. Our dear friend Russell had died during the night.

I had bought the business of Hitchcock's Funeral Directors in the East End from Russell, an old friend and a wonderful character, some four years earlier. Russell and I had had a long conversation just a day or two before his death. He had been unwell in hospital, but after I had spoken to him for an hour or so he was cheerful and, I felt, getting better. So hearing of his death – and over the telephone, the worst way you could possibly be told – collected all the dreadful feelings of bereavement around me, reminding me of my mother's death and my feelings at that horrendous moment. Who counsels the counsellor? What happens when your own barriers are down? Does that make you vulnerable or simply human? Does it make your job harder to do, or is it impossible to do properly without those feelings? As a funeral director, you do not have to feel the pain all the time, but you do have to understand it to be truly helpful to others.

I sat in solemn silence in my office reflecting on my friendship with Russell and the experiences we have shared together. Conversation, laughter, a drink or two and, most of all, trust. Russell had entrusted me with his business. He had recently not felt well enough or able enough to continue running it himself and did not want to sell to anyone but me, which warmed me and filled me with emotion when I thought about his confidence in me. Russell was very much part of our firm and family. As we say, Russell was in the circle of trust, and losing Russell had fractured that circle. Already my mind was busy trying to cement it back together – that's just survival, but nature.

I quickly rang round to let everybody know what had happened and went personally over to Harlow, where Russell had been in a private hospital, to bring him home. It was a quiet and thoughtful journey to Harlow, and upon my arrival I was confronted with the feeling that seeing is believing. Then, as I was looking at Russell, I realised that the worry and pain had gone from his face and he finally looked at peace. Russell had had diabetes for many years, and his organs were just giving up on him. It was clear at that moment that there would be no more pain for Russell. No more loneliness (because Russell had lived alone). He was truly at peace, and I could see that. On my way back, with Russell just at the side of me, it was as if we were sharing a conversation in my mind. I could hear his laughter, see his smile and reflect on his philosophy of life.

Then suddenly I felt a dreadful emptiness that these thoughts would not stay with me. New laughter and new conversations would not be shared, and there was a terrible gripping in my stomach and palpitations in my heart. I knew that I had to write down what was going through my mind. I needed to describe bereavement in a simple way that everybody could understand, and this is what I came up with. If it helps one person, it has been worth writing.

Imagine this if you can. Picture yourself standing on a small island late at night in the cold depths of winter. There is no moon, there is no sight of land anywhere, it is getting darker and colder. In the distance, you can hear and see the beginning of a storm that extends with no apparent end. You are hungry and afraid, but worst of all you are alone and can see no way out. Can you imagine the terror of that feeling? If you can and your heart is pounding and your stomach twisting, you are just beginning to feel the first pangs of bereavement.

But that is just the beginning: it doesn't end there. Now imagine that the person who has always been there for you, who has always been your comfort in life, is just in front of you. You can see them but you cannot touch them, cannot reach them, cannot speak to them, and that person has no knowledge of your existence. *That* is the emptiness of bereavement. You can see no hope, no future. Those terrible feelings will depress you, and with that depression could come illness, heartbreak and dreadful loneliness. Frightening, isn't it? It sounds and feels hopeless, and on top of all that your memories become confused, and the added fear of losing them is the final straw.

I remember, when my mother died, the heartache of trying to remember her smell, her face, her hair, her voice. In reality, I was not trying to remember, but trying never to forget. These thoughts and memories of Mum were recently brought streaming back to me when a seventeen-year-old boy spoke at his mum's funeral of his own fears. He was incredible and left all of us a little tearful. You see, you are always vulnerable – always.

We feel almost disloyal if we forget one thing about the person we have lost, but that confusion is short-lived, and as the months and years go by you begin to realise that all those memories are within you and nobody can take them away. That person is a part of you, so that something always remains within you. It becomes a great comfort: your pain eases and your memories become a wonderful reflection of reality. In our minds, we have a photograph album. Each page we turn is a memory we revisit, and in time the pain eases and the memories become a comfort. We begin to realise that there really is a way forward and a purpose for living the life we have left.

This might sound strange, but just writing this description of bereavement has given me much comfort in my grief over Russell's death. Of course, losing a friend like Russell (however tragic and sad) was not like losing Mum. But the feelings of grief surrounding Russell's death have lifted the barrier and allowed the pain of Mum's death to revisit me from a long time ago. I clearly understand that bereavement is an illness – for some only like a cold, for others pneumonia – and when we understand that, we will all realise that there is great hope for the future.

So there you are, on this island, completely desperate, but just as you think that despair can never be overcome, the storm turns, the cold begins to lift, morning supersedes the darkness of the night and you notice that the rain from the storm has brought fresh water to drink. As the light allows you to see the small island clearly, you notice fruit to eat on bushes and trees that you were not even aware were there. Then, feeling a little better with each find, you notice on the horizon a boat – refuge, safety, help – and in that boat smiling faces and people you know who are pleased to see you.

Imagine the joy, the relief and the comfort of familiarity and safety. You gradually begin to realise that life still has so much left, but as you step on to the boat and look back towards the island, the fear you have been feeling briefly touches you again. Even though you have left the island, this will still be the case from time to time in your dreams, but then you enter clearly back into the world and you no longer feel alone. This time, when we see our loved one in front of us, they are reaching us when we thought we could not reach them. We are comforted by the occasional familiar smell, a similar voice, laughter from an old joke we have shared together, a prayer we might whisper. We are aglow with the force of life that person has left with us, making our memories now warm and no longer cold. The dead never leave us: they are a force that is constantly with us.

We never get over losing somebody, but we learn to live our lives alongside our pain. Bereavement changes us for ever. We never forget – we never could – but we cope and we can be happy again. Through our own hopes, we can then help each other to continue to enjoy every taste, every adventure, every experience that life has left for us, often in honour of the person we have lost. Life in itself is a true possession – live it! That is the job for us ourselves, our families and our friends as human beings. We are all likely to face such a situation, but face it we will, and move on we will. As the poem in Chapter 5 said, remember that parting is hell but life goes on, so smile.

Growing old and approaching death can be a frightening experience for us all. You will have seen from my picture that I have greyish-white hair. People have often asked whether I have thought of dyeing my hair, but I would sooner be permanently grey than permanently orange, and to be honest grey hair is much more distinguished – well, that's my excuse anyway, that's how I see it. They say that men's minds work 4 per cent more quickly than women's, but, in defence of women I think that only applies to sex, don't you? So much of what we are – our culture, childhood, upbringing, nationality – directs the way in which we think and the way in which we see things.

Take the American lady who arrived at Heathrow and stayed a couple of days nearby in a hotel. During her visit, she toured beautiful Windsor Castle. When she returned home and was describing her trip to her friends, she commented, 'You know, I can't understand why such a beautiful castle was built so close to an airport. The British are very strange people, you know.' So you see, we shouldn't comment unless we can see the whole picture (or know a little more about history!).

Often the first ones to see the whole picture surrounding bereavement are, believe it or not, children. So how do children cope with bereavement? Well, a lot better than adults give them credit for, I promise you. It is my view that we should never close doors to them. Never leave them out of the experience of losing somebody. If they are old enough to ask you about death, they are old enough to be sharing the experience of it. Don't turn them away.

A brilliant illustration of this happened recently when we met a mum and dad who had brought their children along with them to make the arrangements for Nanny Nora's funeral. There was an older child, Robert, and then there was Tim, who was five. Mum and Dad were great, speaking to Robert and Tim and including them in all the arrangements. There were no secrets, no closed doors as I call them. We asked Dad what he would like to do with the ashes after the cremation: 'Well, I think we would like to take them somewhere that she really liked.'

At this point, Robert piped up, 'Ooh, ooh, Dad, I know – let's take them to Marks & Spencer's. Mum, Dad, let's take them there.'

'I don't think Marks & Spencer's would like that very much, Robert,' said Dad. 'I don't think they would let us do that.'

'Well, Dad, do you remember *The Great Escape*, that film we watched? We could put holes in our pockets, and we could walk around Marks & Spencer's pouring the ashes from our pockets and nobody would notice, Dad.'

Everybody laughed at this point. This little lad was very much part of his nanny's funeral, and when they all went in finally to say goodbye to their nanny, Robert could be heard saying, 'Bye, Nanny Nora, I'll see you in about eighty years, then.' (How wonderful!)

Children know far more than we give them credit for. This remarkable young man was already coming to terms with the loss and doing his best to involve himself in the family experience because that is how he saw it. He was going to miss his nanny and would never forget her. I must admit this is a remarkable young man, but aren't all children remarkable given the chance?

Robert's mum contacted us several times after the funeral to thank us and to tell us how the children were getting on and how they were all rebuilding their lives after the loss. One story related to the children and their grandad. It seems that the boys helped him with the lighter work in his garden, and Grandad, mindful of Tim being young, said that one day he would be able to help with the heavy work too. Robert looked up at him, scratched the top of his head (a bit like Laurel and Hardy, I think) and said, 'You'll be dead then, Grandad.' There was an awful silence – the kind of silence when you cannot believe what you have just heard – at which point Grandad fell about laughing and said, 'Do you know what, Robert, you are probably right, young man, but until then I will find you a lighter job, something we can all do together, boys.'

Children say the most innocent and funny things, don't they? We need to listen to them and sometimes to learn from them too. But most of all, as ever, we need to love them. If children can cope with loss and bereavement, and I know that with help they can, then surely – following our train of thought from the start of the chapter – we should be able to cope with the loss of a child. But can we?

For so many, it is a dreadful case of having to cope. I would never be impertinent enough to tell anybody who had lost a child that I knew how they felt because I had seen it in other people a thousand times. How could I know? I have never lost a child, thank God. All I know is that it does not get any worse than this. This is as bad as it can be. Only comfort and time can plaster over the wound, that much I know. I know how important the funeral is in dealing with any loss, but I feel it is particularly important with the loss of a child for the parents to take every possible active part in that funeral. Taking personal time to say goodbye, perhaps holding the child, carrying the child on the day of the funeral, writing something about your loss – and if you can dig deep inside and find the courage to read it, you can in some small way share your grief with others. Saying goodbye is so terribly hard – believe me, it seems impossible – but letting go gently in time is a reality.

Many people think that support means lightening the sorrow, perhaps wiping away the tears. Even if that support does not help the loss, it can and often does help the loneliness. Even someone *giving* support is just as helpless as the person who is in mourning, and if you are truly trying to share a loss together, often the only way you can do this is by just being there. You can become an unmoveable tower of strength, perhaps the only trustworthy element in somebody's damaged world. That trust is, however, an enormous responsibility to the bearer as it has to be continuous – not just there for a moment or a day. Nothing depicts friendship more truly than supporting a friend through bereavement. To both parties, it is a true gift.

So how important is the funeral itself? It is a necessary ritual, and being part of it is an essential part of self-repair. My professional advice to anybody who has had a loss is to be as active as you possibly can in the preparation of the funeral and the funeral itself. Try to stay focused at the most essential moments of that day. Take everything in, forget nothing, remember everything. I did this at my mum's funeral and it stood me in good stead. I remember every painful moment, but not now with remorse. The only remorse I have is that I never took a more active part at the time. Perhaps I was too young, and at the time it was not the done thing. I wish I had had the courage to speak or read, but sadly I didn't. At the time, participating seemed so hard, yet it is so rewarding.

I conducted my nan's funeral, which I shall never forget, and I know several priests who have conducted the funerals of their own mother or father, and although this was terribly difficult the moment became a true staff of support to them. Being involved leaves you with a great sense of pride and achievement: you feel that you have done the best you possibly could for the person you have lost. But if you cannot read or take part, don't be ashamed – talk to somebody you trust who will perhaps give a eulogy for you. Tell them what you would like to say yourself – this too will leave a true glow of satisfaction and support for the person you have lost. Don't be afraid to tell your funeral director exactly what you want. However silly it may seem to you, he or she will understand its importance.

My friend Chris Mullane often says that 'Hindsight is a wonderful thing', but take my advice and don't depend on hindsight. Trust your feelings, and do not be ashamed of laughter. Emotions are a mixed bag and show themselves in unusual ways at the most inconvenient times, but then we don't always get it right, do we? When God granted Solomon that which he most desired, Solomon chose wisdom. Was he right? Or should he have chosen money (only joking)? I mention this because, as human beings, we often do not really know what we want from life. So how are we going to be any better in knowing what we want from death? It is going to be a shock, and we should not rush it.

Take time and think it all out clearly. Talk to your family, if you have one, or to friends. In this day and age, funerals do not have to be rushed. There are those who believe the funeral should take place almost immediately. This tradition has its roots in sensible hygiene practices, but modern technology has now granted us more time. Not meaning to be disrespectful, but I suppose that the deceased is not going to get any better, so we might as well go ahead and get on with it. But there is so much to prepare, after all. A wedding may take up to two years to prepare, and do you think a funeral is any less important? There is so much to do – people to tell and invite, churches to find, cars to book, coffins to choose, flowers, catering, memorialisation, visiting, time to say goodbye, condolence books, music – it goes on and on. Yet we may have only days, a week or two at the most, and all of this comes at a time when we are bereaved. Making yourself busy with arrangements is good for you as it carries you through that difficult time.

I have found that the final stage of the grief circle is acceptance, and the funeral is often the first step towards that acceptance. The brilliant doctor Elisabeth Kübler-Ross remarked on the similarity of the grief circles for those who learn that they are terminally ill and those who have suffered the death of a family member. Doctor Ross believes that the grief circle goes through stages of shock, denial, anger, mourning and recovery, the latter only coming with acceptance. And what does recovery mean? In truth, we never recover from loss. Death changes our lives for ever. Things may never be perfect again, and although it is true to say that the pain of death will diminish in time, it never truly goes away in its entirety. We will always long for the person whom we truly loved, but we will, given the chance and with help, re-establish our lives and move on.

Make no mistake, however: bereavement is a sickness, an illness. In this country, we do not perhaps recognise that clearly enough. I have mounted a lifetime campaign against bereavement and its dreadful effects. It can cause physical pain, somatic distress, tightness of the throat, a choking feeling, shortness of breath, palpitations, sighing, empty feelings in the stomach, cramps, loss of strength, tension, guilt, hostility, restlessness, aimlessness, loss of concentration. Through our weakness, we may even reflect signs and symptoms in ourselves similar to those our loved ones may have died with, such is the power of this dreadful thing.

You see, grief hurts. When we refer to the pain of grief, that pain is real. Grief is an emotional hurt needing healing just as we heal from a physical wound. Many real physical diseases and much mental illness can be traced to grief. A famous author (much more famous than me) has compared grief with peeling an onion, in that it comes in layers and you cry a lot. But I believe memory will also provide us with

201

much laughter, and that laughter is grief's biggest enemy. Use it well, though, because grief is very personal, and everyone must heal in their own way and in their own time.

What I have given you here are not magical solutions or absolutes but only guidelines. There is no amazing point on anyone's calendar when grief is overcome, but overcome it will be with kindness, help and belief. I always ask bereaved people whether they have seen their doctor, and if they have not, I recommend that they do. We all need some physical help and should not be ashamed of that. For a while, the journey is too painful to make on our own. For a while, we may need something to help us sleep, maybe just a few vitamins to give us a lift, sometimes referral to a counsellor for help. Above all, your doctor will need to know what has happened to you and your family so that they can keep an eye on you and be aware of what you may be going through: if they don't know, they can't help. From time to time, they may just give you a call or check up on you, and they may be able to offer you some gentle advice or care when it is most needed.

Bereavement is often known as the 'thirteen-month illness', in that we need to pass every anniversary to be able to look forward again. To me the stages are numbness, denial, deprivation, depression and finally acceptance.

I have said much in this chapter about loss and bereavement. Some of the things may have left you a little afraid, but I hope that they have left you comforted too. Never give up and never give in. Get up each day, is my best advice. Put one foot in front of the other and see what the day brings. A footstep may take you forwards or backwards, but it always takes you on a journey. This journey can bring a new beginning and a new phase of your life that may also contain hope, happiness, love and the strength that we all need to live through this life that we have been given. At the end of this book, there is much practical health and information about the stages of grief – the thirteen-month illness that bereavement represents. For now, though, I would like to leave you with a poem that was recently read at a funeral – a person's last words to their family. These are wonderful words full of real happiness and real hope.

I would like the memory of me to be a happy one
I would like to leave an afterglow of smiles when life is
*   done*
I would like to leave an echo whispering softly down the
*   ways*
Of happy times and laughing times and bright and sunny
*   days*
I would like the tears of those who grieve to dry before the
*   sun.*

10

WHEN DISASTER STRIKES

A mother's story at the funeral of her child

When we took baby Sam from the cold of England which so affected his chest to settle in the wonderful climate and beautiful surroundings of Sri Lanka, we could not even imagine what lay in front of us. How Sam enjoyed this beautiful country. His dad and I and the children would sit every morning in the beautiful sunshine enjoying breakfast together with all the time in the world to play with Sam, and as the evenings approached and the sun began to set – such beauty. We had never been happier and I truly thought that life does not get better than this. Christmas had just passed: it was Boxing Day, 26 December 2004. We had taken a picnic to the beach and were all enjoying the sunshine, peace and tranquillity of this beautiful country where the people are so kind, the food so wonderful and everything was perfect. All was right with the world until a wave thirty feet high travelling at 200 miles an hour took Sam from my arms and from our lives. We desperately tried to recover Sam, and his father eventually grasped him into his arms. We tried so hard, Sam, to breathe life back into you, but it was too late: water had filled your lungs and you had died quietly in your father's arms. All that was good now seemed so wrong, so bad. All around us was devastation and death. This peaceful land, these quiet people, their lives destroyed as now ours had been. Thousands dead. The local children's school washed completely into the sea, gone for ever, as were the children. Our dear friend and colleague in Sri Lanka, his whole life turned inside out and his own child lost, yet he was still trying to help us as so many others were. They were constantly grieving with us and apologising for this dreadful disaster which was never of their doing, yet still they felt responsible for us. With the help of the British Consul, the Coroner, the funeral directors, the Sri Lanka government, we were able to bring Sam back to England. To you, John and Sally, our two darling children, thank you so much for living. Thank you so much for surviving. Sam can feel no pain now, he died completely innocent. He was a perfect child. Perfectly loved. We have pledged, my husband and I and our children, to raise as much money as we possibly can to help rebuild the school in Sri Lanka.

We will go back. We will begin our lives again. We will help our friends rebuild. We will never forget you, Sam, how could we?

We all sat in tears at the crematorium while we listened to a beautiful song that the family had chosen. The woman's husband reiterated the whole story with such tender love and care, compassion and strength. I have never seen two such incredible parents and their two lovely children who had tried so hard to live when Sam had failed because of his frailty: he was just eight weeks old.

In all my life as a funeral director, I have witnessed great courage, true passion but never such strength, passion and courage put together in one family. Through the mother's tears, which she shed throughout her speech, all of us there who witnessed her wonderful words were transported to that country so harshly treated by nature and, for just a moment, were able to share the happiness and sadness of their lives since they had moved there. This family inspired me; they inspired everybody in that crematorium. I hope to God that they will have the strength and courage to continue their struggle with bereavement and that, through their dreadful loss, others will benefit from their strength. It is so hard to believe that out of such peace and tranquillity can come such a dreadful wave, the wave they call a tsunami, and that its devastation changes the lives of thousands in a moment.

Back here in England, as we witnessed the aftermath of

this event on TV, we could not begin to imagine the immense damage and loss of life that had been suffered from that one brief instance, and as the death toll rose day by day, the true horror of what had happened began to hit home. Never before has the world gathered together so much charitable help and kindness at one moment. On the scene were such wonderful organisations as Oxfam and Cafod, and most of the world's governments offered immediate help. There were airlifts, fresh water, blankets, tents and endless volunteers, yet to begin with nothing was enough as the devastation continued to unfold.

But what was the role of the undertaker in all this? Is this the time that we became one of the emergency services ourselves? Little do people know of the work we often do. Within hours of this disaster striking, phones were ringing all round the country. Disaster teams were being put together that included embalmers, funeral directors, repatriation experts, DNA experts and disaster co-ordinators.

Our first call came from our sister company (as, unofficially, we like to refer to them), Kenyon Emergency Services. (We are the joint owners of Kenyon Christopher Henley Limited, probably the biggest disaster co-ordinators and repatriators in the world.) Within hours, my colleague Christopher Henley was on his way to Thailand. For him, this was a particularly personal disaster as he is married to a Thai lady and has Thai family. We were busy here organising back-up teams and stand-by help. In charge of the team based in Thailand was the incredible and very experienced Bob Jenson, who contacted me to ask whether I would speak to members of the British government in the UK to try to co-ordinate an emergency mortuary out in Thailand and Sri Lanka. After the political toing and froing that is of course inevitable in these situations, he achieved this. Within days, the whole Kenyon team was out there, with back-up in place in the UK, as it was in America and Australia.

On 27 December, my son Simon had received a phone call and was busily trying to get a number of mobile phones shipped out for use by the disaster team. He was also asked to provide forty to fifty emergency embalming tables, which all had to be collapsible. Now there is no such a thing, but with the help of our dear friend Richard Arnold, under-lining the fact that it's not what you know but who you know that matters, fifty tables were immediately put under construction. The legs were cut off pre-made tables, hinged and made collapsible, the whole lot being wrapped and delivered within twenty-four hours to a relief aircraft. I still do not know how Simon and Richard achieved this, but achieve it they did. Other equipment required, such as disaster bags, emergency back-up equipment, the mobile phones, tables, you name it, was obtained one way or another by someone on the international team.

As I write this chapter, some two months after the disaster, the team is still working out in Thailand, Christopher having had only a week's break. We are still constantly in communication with Bob Jenson and the team, and repatriation is still occurring, though only at a trickle. The true horror of this disaster lies in the fact that so many people are still unidentified, demanding the vigorous use of DNA testing and meaning that people are still awaiting the repatriation of their loved ones. I am sure this will go on for months yet, such is the enormity of this task.

Back in England, our National Association are taking a helpful stance raising money to help the Metropolitan Police at Heathrow set up a repatriation co-ordination desk. The West London Coroner was appointed as the Coroner for all deceased people returning to this country, and a mortuary was set up with additional facilities at the Fulham Road Coroner's Court and mortuary, for which we were asked to supply a number of trolleys.

What most people do not realise is that most of the work that we as funeral directors do in disasters is often carried out (as is the case with many companies) at cost or with a loss of income. When disaster strikes, response rather than money is all that matters. Throughout the land, funeral directors joined together to offer their help and facilities. They are a truly brilliant and underrated group of people – unsung heroes, many of them. A relief fund called the Funeral Service Asian Relief Fund was established, many donations being presented to that fund from America, the UK and worldwide. We knew that there would be families returning to the UK bereaved, bewildered, numb, frightened and wanting help. As funeral directors, we had to be ready for action. We had to be patient. We had to be calm. We had, as always, to be here.

It affected us in a personal way too. My cousin was there on holiday and had not been able to ring home for several days, so we were concerned for his safety until we got his call. My partner Jackie's son had been in Phuket only a few days before the disaster struck. She was petrified for his safety. Fortunately, he was quick to ring and let her know all was well, but as human beings we always think the worst, and any disaster becomes so much more personal when we fear that someone we know might be involved.

We were all perhaps more shocked about this disaster than any other because it affected so many different nationalities from around the world and came from nothing on a calm day. We could not ever have imagined such a thing. I think we understand some natural disasters a little better. Air crashes, however dreadful, are not uncommon in our world, but a wave thirty feet high travelling at 200 miles an hour is incomprehensible. I have been told that, only months before, a film had been released in which such a wave hit the American coast, causing devastation and changing the whole world's climate. I guess the people who had seen that film would never have imagined it really happening. It is times like these that we realise how fragile life is. Many people in Asia lost everything – their families, their homes, their businesses. God only knows how these people will ever put one foot in front of the other and start again.

While the world was still reeling from the news of the tsunami and the many tragic stories that arose from it, I received a dreadful call from the Ministry of Defence: a Hercules aircraft had crashed in Iraq with servicemen on board – nine RAF aircrew and an SAS soldier. This was the highest number of British forces lost in one event since the war had begun. Again, the nation was in shock, so shocked in fact that the Prime Minister gave the news in person in a TV interview. He was clearly moved by the loss of these ten good men, and I knew that the coming week or two would be demanding and very important for us here and at Kenyon Christopher Henley.

At the Ministry's request, we immediately sent five of our staff, including DNA testing experts and repatriation experts, out to Iraq, while the remaining staff and I began to prepare for the ceremonial homecomings that would follow. Although, as I said before, I have never carried out a royal funeral, this was to be a top ceremonial, meaning a member of the Royal Family in attendance, with high-ranking government ministers and all the top brass who would accompany such an event. This meant that Princess Anne and her family were to be there, as were Geoff Hoon, field marshals, colonels and other great dignitaries from all the services. We were to provide ten matching hearses, a matching reserve hearse and two other support vehicles for the occasion. Thanks as ever to my friends Peter Hindley, Andrew Davis and the Dignity Group, we were able to obtain nine matching Mercedes hearses, all brand new; the remaining two were to come, with equally grateful thanks, from my friends Norman and Martin Green and their family.

Now, the servicemen were to return to their home base, RAF Lyneham, but our opening day of practice was to take place on the airstrip at Brize Norton. We were told to stand by for the rehearsal on the Sunday, later changed to early on the Monday morning. This was to be a very moving occasion, far more complicated than any ceremonial we had previously undertaken. There were six bearer parties, four of which would each carry two of the deceased. All were smart lads and anxious to do well for the friends whom they had lost. It fell to my old friend Tom (go and read Chapter 7 again if you need reminding!) as Garrison Sergeant Major, and Harry the Warrant Officer, one representing the RAF, the other representing the Army and Ceremonial Department, to train these fine lads, prepare the airfield with markings and be sure that, working together, we made a complete success of the soldiers' homecoming, an honour they indeed deserved.

As ever, we practised and practised and practised. With six teams to train, it was more difficult than ever. We were out on a cold airfield, into the back of a C17, out of the C17, on to the hearse, off the hearse, back to the C17, on and on and on until it was perfect. We then mapped out a plan of how this would work at RAF Lyneham, and late that evening we eventually retired for a meal and our own personal preparation for the day to come.

212

The next morning we were up sharp, bright and early at RAF Lyneham, a hive of activity for the day even though the camp was clearly in mourning. By ten o'clock we had mapped out our route from the hangar, where all hearses were to be kept, coming round one by one past the servicemen, past the families and past the Princess Royal in attendance. Then on past the C17 that was delivering the boys back, and round across the runway to a special hangar that had been prepared as a chapel.

At precisely ten minutes past one, the plane landed. It deflared, and at exactly twenty-five minutes past it taxied round in front of the hangar where the hearses were waiting, gleaming, spotless and ready to go. As it passed the hangar to stop in front of the Princess Royal and the families of the deceased, I began my march, paging the hearses in procession, all ten in a line, with one waiting just by the side of the hangar in case we had a breakdown. The plane came to a standstill, the back opened and around walked Tom, crisply dressed and immaculate, as we all were. Behind him came the bearer parties, one by one.

Tom gave me my main signal to move. With hat, gloves and stick, I quietly paged the first hearse round at a slow walking pace until I got to my spot just in front of the Princess Royal. I turned, walked to the hearse, handed my gloves, stick and hat to the driver, went to the rear, opened the hearse and stood silently as the first coffin was taken ceremonially from the back of the C17 to solemn music from the RAF band. It was moving, emotional and quite beautiful, really. From the corner of my eye I could see the Princess Royal motionless, immaculate and respectful, and the tears from the surrounding families. The first coffin was placed on to the hearse and the back door closed. I walked again to my spot and indicated to my colleague, with just a movement of my head, that the second hearse should move forward. We repeated this slowly over the next hour for all ten repatriated men.

After the last hearse had been filled, I walked to the front and sat next to the driver. Slowly, we made our way past the C17 and around to the private chapel, prepared with flowers, RAF carpet and trestles that had been specially and lovingly made, a beautiful tribute to their colleagues. Here, all ten coffins were laid. We stayed there for four or five hours while the families privately spent some time with their loved ones. Then came the most moving moment of all.

It was now approaching eight o'clock at night and quite dark as we prepared to leave for Swindon Hospital, where the Coroner was to undertake an investigation. We had a lead car with a violet light, followed by all ten hearses plus the last reserve hearse, in case of emergency; the support vehicles were in place. Each coffin was covered, as ever, by a Union Flag, and lights shone brightly on top of the flags, illuminating the coffins in each of the ten hearses. Slowly, we proceeded to the gates of the airbase, with nine police outriders, a BMW police escort car and two other police cars. All the traffic lights were to be stopped for us on our journey.

But what I did not expect as we approached the gates of the airbase was a line of soldiers and RAF colleagues standing to attention and saluting as their colleagues passed. Even more overwhelming, as we turned out of the base for our slow procession through Lyneham, was that the whole town, to a person, seemed to have turned out to say goodbye to these young men. What I suddenly realised was that this tragedy had affected not just the families of the deceased men, not just the military, but in fact the whole country. The people of Lyneham itself stood quietly and emotionally, tearfully in some cases, as we slowly filed past them. For miles, the people stood. As the tragedy of the loss of so many young lives hit me, my feelings overcame me, a tear or two leaving my eyes and a lump appearing in my throat.

I will never forget that evening or the people of Lyneham. This had started off as a Royal Ceremonial for me, but I suddenly realised that that was unimportant. What mattered was the emotion of everyday people. The respect from the Royal Family, the government, the Ministry of Defence and the armed forces had been immaculate, but the love of the people who lined the roads, and of the families of the deceased, was clearly overwhelming – a moment I shall never forget as long as I live.

So, when a disaster hits, whether it is a tragedy of war, a tsunami, an earthquake, bringing death in an instant, often to so many, backing up the aid agencies and the governments will be the funeral directors. Always anxious to help, always ready to undertake the worst jobs in the most dreadful conditions and always ready to join together in a spirit of oneness and support for those in need. Strong shoulders when they are needed the most.

Sometimes in life, as we know, things don't run smoothly. In business, believe me, if you are to be successful, you probably fail more often than you will succeed – because if you never try the difficult route, you may never achieve anything really special. I have been working for the past two years on the possibility of a hand-built fleet of custom-made cars for Albin's. Having taken this arduous route, disaster struck today. The company that has been working so hard to produce the cars for me may have to go into voluntary liquidation, which means we may only get part of our fleet or have to redirect our efforts – more money and more work to achieve something special.

With my sons, all of us feeling rather sorry for ourselves, I was reflecting on what we had lost financially and trying to find a way forward when it struck me that this was nothing but a setback, a change of plan. I have just written about true disasters (so what was I thinking?) and what would people who have suffered from them give to be in my position now? I immediately saw that this was nothing in comparison and that what I had to do was make the best of a bad situation. For every negative, there is a positive.

At the start of this chapter, that lovely mother was already inspiring me to the reality of life and death and what really matters, so I will pick myself up, make the best of things and give Albin's the fleet it still deserves – we are on the case to achieve it, believe me. You would have to walk in another person's shoes to know how disaster actually feels, and we really are 'the lucky ones'.

11

DON'T YOU JUST LOVE
YOUR JOB?

I have always said to my sons that the job that I do, and that
we all now do, is the greatest job in the world if you are
doing it to please yourself. If, however, you are doing it to
please somebody else (your father for example!), the burden
and responsibility of such a mantle would be too hard to
carry for the duration. Interestingly, both my sons have
chosen to follow me into this profession, a decision that has
been totally theirs to take.

   People think that being a funeral director is a depressing
occupation. Far from it! It is a rewarding and a wonderfully
warm profession that we belong to. You see, at the most
difficult times in people's lives, we are invited close into
their lives as funeral directors. We are invited to be part of
their family for a short time. We have the opportunity to
bring comfort, security, compassion and care, and to me my
work is a true possession. You will also know, by having read
my previous chapters, that it has its very amusing moments

and that funeral directors are anything but depressing people.

Since we made the television programme *Don't Drop the Coffin*, it has not been unusual for a family to come to us because they saw us on the TV, perhaps also asking that I conduct the funeral, as I appeared most often in the documentary. This happened recently when I was asked to conduct a funeral in Brixton. As the cortège pulled up outside the house, I heard a group of girls who were attending the funeral gossiping: 'He's the bloke off that television programme.'

'Is he?' they said. 'Which programme's that?'

'You know, that *Six Feet Under*.'

'Oh yeah.'

Not quite! *Six Feet Under* is a fictional American TV programme depicting a family firm of West Coast funeral directors, in which the plot is complicated by the fact that one of the sons is straight and the other is gay. (I wonder which one they thought I was!)

But it gets more tenuous. Returning to the office one afternoon from conducting a funeral, I went into the reception area of Albin's. I smiled pleasantly at a group there who were waiting to arrange a funeral, and wished them good afternoon. One lady said, 'He's the bloke from that programme, ain't he, you know, *Don't Drop the Dead Donkey*.'

'No, darling,' I said, 'you mean *Don't Drop the Coffin. Don't Drop the Dead Donkey* is something completely different.'

Her family immediately saw the mistake and rolled up with laughter. 'Mum, it's not even called that – it's called *Drop the Dead Donkey*, not *Don't Drop the Dead Donkey*, you silly thing! Barry's programme was *Don't Drop the Coffin* – remember?'

'Oh, yes,' Mum said. 'I remember – *Don't Drop the Coffee*, that's it.'

Well, at least it broke the ice for everyone. But *Don't Drop the Coffee* – what next?

I have also been accused of looking like Pete Waterman. Now that's really not funny! *Don't Drop the Dead Donkey*, *Six Feet Under*, but not Pete Waterman, please (no offence, Pete, but you wouldn't want a look-alike either). But as my mum used to say, I don't care what people call me as long as they don't call me late for dinner. After all, by any other name I am the same person.

The recent interest in TV programmes such as *Six Feet Under*, *William and Mary* and our own documentary *Don't Drop the Coffin* have led to more interest in the funeral industry and more youngsters wanting to become members of our profession. It is certainly about time that our profile was raised. It is an honourable profession and a wonderful club to belong to, particularly at Albin's, where we pride ourselves on teamwork. I have often heard it said that multiple chains are soulless, but surely that could also be said about some smaller individual firms. Being small, as I have often said, does not give you the monopoly on care. There are many managers who are excellent funeral directors, and many operatives in the larger companies who try very hard to get things right. I think you have to judge everybody and each firm on its merits. Funeral directors in general are good people.

The wonderful programme *William and Mary* revolves around a funeral director and a midwife who fall in love. It was warm and encouraging to read a newspaper article by Lynda Lee-Potter:

ITV: beguiling *William and Mary* back on Sunday nights with Martin Clunes as a funeral director.

Script writer Mick Ford says: 'I wanted William to be the sort of undertaker we would all like to come into contact with when necessary.

'William is humane but also true to life. When my father died in the middle of the night the scruffy duty doctor was indifferent and uncaring and called the police without even telling me. The police officers who came to the house were graceless. My father's GP chillingly insisted on a post-mortem examination though my father was eighty-nine years old and had died from an aneurysm. However, the young undertaker was infinitely patient, compassionate and a constant support. He organised the funeral with dignity and the impeccable timing of a perfectionist.

'I thought that I had been merely lucky but talking to people since I have discovered that they have had similar experiences with undertakers across the land.

'The medical profession would do well to pick up a
few tips from their dedication and kindness.'

What a lovely article! You see, this is commonplace in my
experience – funeral directors are all those things and more.

Some of the funniest things happen on funerals too.
Take, for example, a funeral that we recently conducted
where a gentleman was following the hearse in his own car.
He got caught at the lights and unfortunately took the
wrong turning. He then saw, going across the traffic lights
on Jamaica Road, Bermondsey, what he thought was the
hearse from the funeral he had been following. Unfortunately, it was another one of my hearses going to a funeral
in a completely different direction. He followed this hearse
for some miles before noticing, as it turned left, that the
name on the side was 'Ethel', whereas the name on the side
of the hearse he had been following was 'George'. So there
he was, following completely the wrong funeral. Luckily, he
was able to phone my office after realising his mistake and
correctly divert to the crematorium where George's funeral
was taking place – he made it just in time. After the funeral,
even he had to have a giggle with us: 'What a coincidence!'
he said. 'One minute I'm following George, the next minute
I'm following Ethel: I must have been lost somewhere in my
head mentally.'

If you have read my other books, you will know that I
have a habit of falling over. I can't help it; I don't know how
it happens, there is usually nobody near me. On this

occasion we were at the Honor Oak Crematorium. We had removed the coffin carrying the deceased from the back of the hearse. I was standing at the foot of the coffin walking backwards up the slope and directing everybody to follow me, arms out wide and Father Alan just in front of me walking up the slope. For some reason, he stopped for a moment, I put my heel on the back of his heel, completely lost my balance and went down with a spectacular wallop on the floor. Like a true professional, I bounced straight back up and continued my work, but not without a huge gasp from the relatives (and a little winding on my part). As is quite usual in Bermondsey, the family were friendly and also worried for my welfare, although I must say that they had a few smiles on their faces at this.

I maintain to this day that Father Alan in fact had me over, but he is claiming he had nothing to do with it at all. Danny Hodges, an old friend of mine and a typical Bermondsey lad, one of the best, said, 'Barry, that's the third time I've seen you fall over on a funeral, mate. I must be a bock; does it only happen when I'm here?'

'No, Danny,' I said, 'I don't need your help. I can fall over all on my own, thanks very much.'

Last year, we conducted a funeral in Bermondsey in which the deceased's first name was Bill and his second name John. By a remarkable coincidence, there was a horse running that day called Sloppy John Bill. The family insisted that we walk from the house with the funeral along Jamaica Road and stop at the betting office while one of the elder sons got out of the car, went inside and put a £10 bet on Sloppy John Bill to win. He came out with the betting slip and put it on Dad's coffin on the hearse (the things people do – lovely, really). Unfortunately, the horse came second, which was a big let-down to the family on the day as to them Bill had always come first. If the horse had won, goodness knows how they would have claimed the winnings, though, as the ticket had been cremated with Dad.

At another funeral, the man concerned was both mum and dad to his boys. It was a wonderful funeral. He was to be placed on the back of an open-backed lorry, one that he himself had driven for many years. It was a real celebration of his life. Hundreds of people followed the funeral as we walked a great deal of the way, past his local betting office, stopping at his local pub and again outside his own house where his sons went into the house to collect his dog, a vicious-looking Rottweiler. They walked with this Rottweiler directly in front of me, ahead of Dad's 'hearse' – the lorry. As I walked behind the dog with my stick, I was in fact a little afraid (of the dog, that is). We came to a crossroads, and the man with the dog stopped and turned, with me still walking directly behind. The dog took one look at me and leapt, snapping only an inch away from my vital areas. It was all the lad could do to hold on to the dog before he got a large helping of me – well, that's my story.

As we turned to the left, the man with the dog walked off to the right and allowed us to process on to the cemetery. I have to confess I was more than a little relieved to see the dog depart, but it was a lovely funeral full of endless love from his family, definitely one to remember. You do not get many hearses in the shape of an open-backed lorry, and that family had made that funeral beautiful on the day. Never underestimate how important it is to have a funeral how you want it to be. For them, Dad was everything, and they proved it that day. Lovely music, doves released and a tree to be planted in the garden – fantastic.

We picked up another funeral at Sidcup recently, backing into a little cul-de-sac with a hearse and four limousines. There were masses of flowers – lots of name displays and tall arrangements – and we had arranged them beautifully on top of the hearse. There was no problem backing into the close, but leaving the close – well! It was summertime, and it was evident that the many hanging branches on the trees would damage the flowers as we proceeded from the close. So we took action. We tied straps to the branches of the trees and pulled them gently back down just enough to secure them, tying them to the bottom of the trees so that the funeral could proceed without damaging either the flowers or the trees. It worked perfectly: the hearse and the cars proceeded while Neil made sure everything was clear for us to get out.

Just as the last limousine passed, however, one strap slipped and the branch of the tree sprung outwards, hitting Neil on the back of the head. Now you have to remember here that Neil is a very good goalkeeper and a bit of a trapeze artist really. He hit the floor as if he had been shot by a sniper, bouncing back up to his feet and rubbing his head, a bit bewildered and embarrassed at what had happened but with a little grin on his face. Everybody, including the mourners, had a little smile at Neil's antics. You really never know what is going to happen next at a funeral.

I recently received something through the post from a company called Celebrities at Peace – it was what they called 'an opportunity'. I quote:

Dear friend,

We would like to introduce you to an exciting opportunity offering a service to your clients which is proving to be very successful. 'Celebrities at Peace' offers a unique funeral service for unique people. Clients who have adored or even emulated their favourite stars can find a final resting place as their heroes. We have a full colour brochure of over 74 stars from which your clients/family can choose. We will also endeavour to develop a new celebrity style should your family wish. Tony our cosmetic designer has many years of experience. After leaving a make up firm she went on to work on productions including *Steel Magnolias* and ITV's *Cracker* and *Vanessa* before retraining and gaining a recognised qualification with the British Institute of Embalmers. Attached are modelled four examples of our work. If you have any further questions or would be interested in booking a presentation please do not hesitate to contact us.

Sincerely,
Managing Director

Attached to this were four photographs of the same lady, of late middle age, depicting her in turn as Britney Spears, Liza Minelli, Liz Taylor and Madonna – none of whom could be recognised as their namesakes, I have to say. You never know what you are going to receive as a funeral director, and I couldn't imagine for a moment, with all my experience in the profession, that anyone would want to look like these people in death. How strange. This certainly left me gobsmacked.

My very good friend Richard Arnold, who is a wonderful embalmer, recently had a funny experience when he was ordering a catalogue from a mail order company that had gone into business supplying funeral goods. Having ordered the full catalogue that the company provided on the Internet, he was more than a little surprised, after looking at serious pages full of funeral handles, crucifixes, interiors, etc., suddenly to find a page of sexual aids. The company supply a lot more than funeral equipment (a *lot* more, obviously). Richard said that he didn't buy anything – well, I believe you, Richard, even if thousands don't. I hoped he checked his product leaflets before he sent them out, although a bit of extra equipment might have increased his business!

I like to say that we are a team at Albin's – but more than that, we are also a team of characters. Last year I went to the England vs Ireland rugby match at Twickenham with my old friend Peter Hindley. Lee was due to pick me up after the game by the main roundabout at Twickenham Road. I couldn't see him when I came out so I phoned his mobile: 'Lee, where are you?'

'I'm about three or four hundred yards up the road from the roundabout, but I can't get any closer – the traffic's terrible.'

'Okay,' I said, 'I'll walk up towards you. Whereabouts are you?'

'I'm not sure,' replied Lee.

'Well, give me a landmark.'

'I'm just behind a White Rose lorry.' Thinking of the white shirts of England and the red rose of England, I decided that he was behind some sort of publicity lorry for the English rugby game. 'I can't see it, Lee,' I said, running quickly up the road towards where I thought he was.

'I'm right behind the lorry,' he repeated.

As I got nearer I realised his mistake: 'That's a Waitrose lorry, you idiot, not a White Rose lorry.'

'Whatever it is, Bal, I'm still behind it!' he said. The Bermondsey cheek of it.

The Fisher Club in Bermondsey was originally a boxing club, and a world-famous one, too, with lots of champions to its name. There were two local lads who boxed, twins like the Cooper brothers. These lads are the Oulds, and they won't mind me using their names because they are good pals of mine – David and Johnny, gentle giants and good fighters in their day too. As they got on a little in years, both turned from their boxing exploits to doing a bit of TV work, acting as bouncers and would-be villains in television programmes. They were tailor-made for it. At their aunt's funeral a few years ago, they told me about one audition. This was an advert for peanuts, and one of the things they had to do on this peanut advert was cry. They sat down in front of the guy who wanted a set of twins who could cry on demand. 'Now, lads,' he said, 'when it comes to the scene where we've got to do the crying, do you think you will be able to manage it?'

They looked at him: 'Cry! Not much, mate, ain't we 'ad enough loss? Ask Albin's the undertakers, they'll tell ya. Cry, that's all we've done the last ten years.'

Sure enough, they got the job and showed they could shed a tear to order. Every time I meet them now, they tell me this story. What a warm-hearted couple of blokes they are – the salt of the earth, and Bermondsey through and through.

We might not be able to shed a tear on demand at Albin's, but one thing that we do often – and well, I think – is to practise. It may be good driving techniques, convoy driving, procedures, car-cleaning – you name it, we practise it. Education is ongoing as ever. One of the more common sights, however, is practising the carrying of coffins through the door of a house with anything from two people right up to ceremonial eights (eight people carrying the coffin). To this end, we have two coffins – one with no weight in it at all, and one that is correctly weighted at about twelve stone. We have spare trestles too, and when I call for a practice, out come the coffins, out come the trestles, the garage is cleared, and behind closed doors we give our young people the opportunity to show us what they can do. As always, we look for new techniques too.

On this particular day it was Dinkle's eighteenth birthday, I seem to remember. We had a cake for him at breakfast and sang the usual 'Happy Birthday', and I told everybody that there would be a carry practice (bearing the coffin on the shoulders) at four o'clock in the afternoon. Sure enough, at four o'clock my boys came to get me from my office. There was the garage cleared, with the practice coffin (now about ten years old), trestles and everything in place. Now, this carry practice was for a particular person who had just joined us and needed to learn some of the finer points of carrying. Quite seriously but with a little bit of humour (like Tom the Garrison Sergeant Major in the ceremonial practices), I began to instruct the practice. The boys were really sharp this day, lifting crisply, turning correctly, reversing, going up and going down when required. This has to be considered because some church doors are so low that if you didn't bob down, all the flowers would come off the coffin.

What I did notice, however, was a little crowd of onlookers at the doorway – Jo, Jackie, Maureen, Steve and one or two others – who were for some reason in hysterics. I'm telling the boys to take no notice of them, it's part of your training to be able to ignore situations around you when you are carrying correctly. So up we went, down we went, the practice lasting for nearly thirty minutes in some shape and form. I turned to the audience and told them to go in and stop disrupting the carry. This of course they did, but within thirty seconds their heads were around the door again. People were making phone calls on their mobiles. In the end, I stopped the practice, put the coffin down and said, 'You've done really well, boys. By the way, where's Dinkle?'

As I said this, the coffin lid opened and out popped Dinkle. 'Here I am, and they're all rubbish, Governor,' were the first words out of his mouth.

Well I never. Dinkle had got himself into the practice coffin and removed the weights. The amazing thing was he didn't make a single sound. Now I understood the phones – the girls were apparently phoning him on his mobile (switched to vibrate rather than ringing) in the coffin and he was whispering to them.

'Are you all right in there?'

'Yeah, it's all right. Very smooth, I thought.'

I suppose you could say that he was able to give me 'inside' information on his chums' carrying abilities. And at least our families can now be assured that we double-check inside and out the suitability of our carrying. Silly boy; I doubt he will ever forget his eighteenth birthday.

I started this chapter by saying my job is, for me, the best job in the world. I am glad, and proud, to say that it seems to be the same for my two sons too. In fact, I think I can extend that belief to everybody who works at Albin's. A proud and wonderful team and a group of people to whom I think you could clearly say, 'Don't you just love your job?'

As I end this chapter, my son Jon and his wife Jane have just told me that – God willing – I am to be a grandad again in September 2005, and I am overjoyed. Another wonderful grandchild to join Olivia and James – who knows whether any of them will find their future in the firm? (I have returned to this chapter a few months later and now Simon and Michelle are, God willing, to have their third child before the end of the year – fantastic!) Can't wait. Life's great!

12

ONE LAST ENCORE

Learn to live well that thou may'st die so too
To live and die is all we have to do.

Or is it? As for me, I intend to live for ever – so far, not bad
at all. For me, there is so much more to life than meets the
eye. We come into this world crying, and it would be nice,
don't you think, to leave it laughing. If my Christian beliefs
surrounding death are correct (not that I want the chance
to find out just yet), believing in our faith is not the final
exit but only a swinging door.

Perhaps Larry Hagman (you know, JR from the TV series
Dallas) has the right idea. What he wants after he dies is
somewhat unusual: 'I would like to be minced and then
spread over half an acre of land. I want to be spread with
some wheat seeds and some marijuana seeds. At the end of
the year, you can harvest me for a huge cake and serve it up
for my birthday. I want a big party for guests to come, and

dancing for three days.' With that kind of cake, Larry, I think three days might not be long enough!

I heard a really good story from a florist recently. It seems that somebody was opening a new business and one of the friends of the new owner wanted to send some flowers for the occasion. When the flowers arrived, the owner of the new business read the card: 'Rest in Peace'. The owner was angry and called the florist to complain, angrily pointing out the obvious mistake. The florist replied (very wittily, I thought), 'Madam, I am really sorry for the mistake, but rather than getting angry you should imagine this – somewhere there is a funeral taking place, and they have flowers with a note saying "Congratulations on your new location".'

My doctor recently told me a less true but nonetheless funny story about a traffic warden. Now, nobody likes traffic wardens, do they? Poor fellows. It seems that this traffic warden had a heart attack while in hospital. The nurse tried to revive him, and the doctor was called. Death was pronounced, and as the doctor went to write out the death certificate he asked the nurse for the full name, the age and the address, all of which he was given. Just as he was being told the occupation, the traffic warden opened his eyes, breathed, asked what was going on and asked the doctor to stop. The doctor replied, 'Sorry, mate, I've already started to write it; you're too late and this time no appeal.' Nice sense of humour, but something tells me this particular doctor must have had a recent run-in with a traffic warden. A timely reminder that humour can heal great wounds.

A very strange thing happened to Jackie and me last Christmas. I had volunteered to go on call with one of the lads. Going on call, of course, requires you, as a funeral director, to be instantly ready to respond to a sudden death. Sure enough, at about eleven o'clock in the evening the phone rang, and we had a call to go out to Sidcup. I met young David at our premises and off we went together, chatting away. As we left the nursing home where we had collected the deceased person, I rang Jackie on my mobile to assure her that I would be back in the next half an hour or so. When we arrived back at our mortuary, we carried out our usual duties, said goodnight and went home. After a reviving cup of tea with Jackie, I turned in.

The next morning, however, I looked everywhere for my phone. I checked my home, my clothes, the vehicle we had used, even David's pockets in case it had ended up in there. I could not find it, yet I knew I had made a call on that phone while sitting in the vehicle – very strange. I assumed that it must have fallen out of my pocket as I got into the car and had either been run over or picked up by somebody else. Either way, I could not trace the phone. Four months down the line, on a Sunday afternoon in late April, Jackie was cleaning out the freezer and, unbelievably, there, in the little pocket at the top of the freezer door, was my phone. As I never go to the freezer, I am still blaming Jackie for putting the phone in the freezer but I cannot imagine how. Naturally, she maintains she has never done such a thing (she would, wouldn't she?). Anyway, somehow it got into the freezer and that's where it was.

I had a chance, though, to try out one of my theories about cryonics. Those of you who have read my other books will know my views on cryonics – I am sure that, one day, we will be able to make parts of deceased people work again, but that memory will never be retained. So I investigated my mobile phone, and with this, at least, I have been proved completely wrong. I charged the phone up, switched it on and there it was, all memory retained – all phone numbers intact and the phone in good working order – so maybe cryonics will one day prove me wrong too. But, Jackie, I still maintain you put that in the freezer (didn't, did, didn't, did, didn't, did, stop it this is silly, yeah OK . . . didn't, did . . .).

The things people do never cease to amaze me. In our funeral journal, I have just read an article from the *Leicester Mail*, dated 4 June 1929. The article comments on the amount of illness caused by funerals or people's attendance of funerals. (It seems that King George fell ill after some exposure to bad weather at the Cenotaph service, which led to this particular article.) It says that standing bare-headed in the cold and the wet opens people up to the awful risk of bad colds and even pneumonia. In other words, what they are really saying is that funerals beget funerals – more serious and fatal illnesses occur in consequence of funerals than any other obligation imposed by society. It is humorous really, isn't it? So no matter how much you care for someone, no matter how much respect you want to show, you shouldn't go really if the weather is bad.

Au contraire, sir – attendance at funerals is important for everybody's health; just wrap up warm. We are in the open day in and day out as funeral directors, and we survive. My lads are the fittest you could find, but then I know that my team of workers are the best. Perhaps we should attend more funerals in the summer because the fresh air and warm sunshine are good for us. You can't win, can you? Let's just get on with life; we'll deal with death when we have to.

The last funeral that I am going to describe in this series of books relates more to a performance than a funeral, one involving some very funny theatrical folks who, in their own special way, created a special funeral – one of the most astonishing I have ever attended. All tradition and convention went out of the window, yet the funeral still represented a wonderful tribute to an incredibly funny man who spent his whole life on the edge. The family have very kindly asked me to use his correct name in telling this story.

The story of Malcolm Hardee, comedian extraordinaire

On the front of the service sheet prepared by the family, there was a picture of Malcolm, glasses pulled down to the end of his nose, eyes looking upwards towards Heaven, top half naked, arms crossed and a set of angel's wings painted on his back. The service sheet opens with, 'You lucky bastard! You have been invited to the service in respect of the

extraordinary & inimitable life of the brilliant Malcolm
Hardee 1950–2005 Rest In Peace 17 February 2005'. I'll print
out the rest for you here so that you can see the incredible
people involved and the enormous length of the service.

Funeral Ceremony
At St Alfege's Church, Greenwich 11.30 a.m.

Walk in Music
(That's Life)

The Coffin is brought into the Church accompanied
by music

Welcome by Father Peter

Hymn Number 1 – All Things Bright and Beautiful
(see Hymn Sheet)

Arthur Smith introduces:

Steve Bowditch
Reads from Luke 6:31–38

Hymn Number 2 – Eternal Father Strong to Save (see
Hymn Sheet)

Frank Hardee

One last encore

Malcolm's son will read a piece he wrote about his dad whilst at school

Stewart Lee
Will make a reading

Jools Holland
Will play Precious Lord Take My Hand

Arthur Smith introduces:

Jo Brand
Who will make a reading

Al Richardson
Will play Harmonica (Malcolm's favourite instrument)

Owen O'Neil
Will read a Poem he has written about Malcolm

Alessandro
Will sing Nessun Dorma, a piece he used to perform with Malcolm whilst naked

Father Peter will perform formal prayers

Some of Malcolm's friends and family will read short tributes

Hymn Number 3 – Jerusalem (see Hymn Sheet)

Father Peter – Blesses the people and performs the
Prayers of Commendation

The coffin will be brought out of the Church
accompanied by a piece of music
chosen by Malcolm before his death

Walking out music
(Return to Sender)

Please all gather outside where balloons will be
released into the air in
Malcolm's memory

Cremation
At Hither Green Crematorium 1.30 p.m.

Music In: 'That's Life' Frank Sinatra

Father Peter performs prayers

The Cremation:
'Hallelujah' – by Jeff Buckley who also drowned in
tragic circumstances

ONE LAST ENCORE

Music Out

Wake at The Trafalgar Tavern
Park Row, Greenwich SE10 9NW

2.00 p.m. – Doors Open

3.00 p.m. – Canapes and finger buffet served

5.30 p.m. – As in Naval tradition a few of Malcolm's
personal artifacts will be
auctioned off

6.30 p.m. – Throwing of wreaths and flowers into his
beloved Thames

Speeches and Music

11.00 p.m. – End

PA supplied out of love and kindness by Music
Rooms
Trafalgar donated free of charge by Frank (The Owner)

'South London's king of comedy, Malcolm Hardee is

a natural clown who in any decent country would be a national institution'
Stewart Lee, *Vox*

'Malcolm was incredible at spotting new talent'
Chris Luby

'A hilarious, anarchic legend; a millennial Falstaff'
Rob Newman

'Raucous, sometimes brutal, often generous'
Dave Cohen

'Godfather to a generation of comic talent
. . . too much of a white-knuckle ride for mainstream programme makers'
Daily Telegraph

'He had the biggest bollocks in show business'
The Guardian

'Past the brute, the blunt and the blunder, we saw the bravest,
the brightest, the best'
Noel Kelly

**A BENEFIT SHOW TO MALCOLM HARDEE
WILL BE HELD AT UP THE CREEK ON
SUNDAY 20 FEB**

HOPE TO SEE YOU THERE

'OY OY'

The funeral was to take place at St Alfege's Church, Greenwich, with the amazing Father Peter taking the service. Now Father Peter was perfect, as they needed a priest who would let things run but also take part in the jokes and be involved in the service in an open and welcoming way. Not pretentious, not overly religious. Father Peter was the perfect person to let the service flow in the way in which the family wanted.

But what about Malcolm? Malcolm was obviously an incredible man: a comedian by profession and once (so I was told) owner of Up the Creek, the comedy club at Greenwich, and the Wibbly Wobbly, the floating pub that was to lead to his final demise. Malcolm lived in a little houseboat a little way down the dock, so he would get in his little rowing boat, row across to the Wibbly Wobbly, have a nice few drinks, get back in the little rowing boat and row home, a little bevy before he went to sleep – lovely! But on this particular evening, Malcolm had spent a marvellous evening on the boat and was much the worse for wear, and disaster fell. Malcolm unfortunately lost his balance, fell into the Thames and was drowned.

Malcolm's lovely family laid out for us exactly how they wanted the funeral to flow, and as ever I was happy to go along with their wishes. In the chapel where Malcolm lay, there was a big rubber ring from the Wibbly Wobbly, and a sailor's hat sat atop his coffin. He was even wearing a sailor suit, or to be precise, a captain's suit. And there was an 'L' plate on the coffin. To my amazement, the first person I took into the chapel was a well-known comedian, a friend of his. He looked straight at him: 'Hello, Malcolm, mate. I'm sorry, boy, I know they're praying for you but I think a rubber ring would have been more help, wouldn't it? Anyway, oy oy, mate' ('oy oy' was Malcolm's signature – how he would announce himself in public life and on stage).

On the day of the funeral, a crisp, bright and sunny February morning, our premises were flooded by well-known faces and people wearing the most amazing clothes, bright and colourful. There was an atmosphere of celebration, with the press present too, and a film crew who were making a documentary in which Malcolm's funeral was to feature. We dealt with hundreds of flowers that were tributes to Malcolm's life and existence – boats, rubber rings, bottles of drink, some very amusing flowers: 'Oy Oy' in letters, Malcolm's name and even one or two other interesting names! As we were carrying Malcolm from our chapel into our garden outside, hundreds of people stood in silence before the shout came, 'Knob out – oy oy!' In my usual conducting fashion, serenely and with features carefully fixed, I carried Malcolm from the front entrance of the chapel, but it was a close thing as I am sure they were determined to make me laugh.

Off we went past the Wibbly Wobbly, round past the streets of Bermondsey and Rotherhithe, on to Deptford and down to Greenwich, where we stopped briefly at the Up the Creek club before reaching the lovely little shop on the corner of the Greenwich one-way system, whose window was displaying a huge picture of Malcolm. We briefly paused again before taking the last journey round the one-way system at Greenwich and on to St Alfege's Church, where hundreds more people were waiting for us.

The church was packed. Jools Holland was sitting waiting to play at his wonderful piano. The sound system was ready, the music in place, the people seated – and in came Malcolm. As we entered the church, we stood for a moment at the entrance while a well-known actor cried the immortal words, 'In show business, we have an old saying. You play St Alfege's Church only twice in your life. On the way up, and on the way down. It's good to be back!' To peals of laughter and the tune 'That's Life', Malcolm entered the church.

Father Peter of course welcomed everybody, and we heard an introduction from the famous – and very funny – comedian Arthur Smith. He and the vicar almost did a double act throughout the service. Arthur started: 'God made the birds and the bees and the flowers, had a couple of pints and then made Malcolm,' adding, 'Sorry, Vicar!' He then asked for a standing ovation for Malcolm's life and that standing ovation must have gone on for as long as five minutes. Whistles, shouts, cries, 'oy oy's everywhere, clapping, laughter and tears – so very moving.

Now, if you have ever been to one of Father Peter's funeral services, you will know that he is very sincere and never leaves the coffin if he can help it: he will try to keep one hand on the coffin and generally kneel throughout. This was quite amusing to some of the comedians. As Arthur got up for the second time to introduce the next speaker, he looked at the priest and said, 'You all right down there on your knees, Vicar?'

Peter got up and immediately replied, 'You're too soon, I'm introducing the next person; stick to the order if you please – sit back down,' to gales of laughter all round. The next time Arthur stood up to introduce somebody, he walked over and said 'And now the Vicar is going to juggle.'

Father Peter just looked: 'What with?'

Next Jools Holland played a wonderful piece, 'Precious Lord, Take My Hand', first solemnly and then in a markedly different tone. There were many wonderful tributes to Malcolm. How he used to write on his tax form 'Deceased' every time it came through, and how it was never unusual for Malcolm to de-clothe himself (hence the 'knob out' comments). In between, we had some traditional hymns – 'All Things Bright and Beautiful', 'Jerusalem', 'Eternal Father, Strong to Save' ('For Those in Peril on the Sea'; 'Very appropriate, don't you think?' said one of his pals) –

sung fantastically by everyone. Jo Brand gave us a short piece she had written, and there were incredible tributes from Malcolm's son and other members of his family. Singer/comedian Alessandro sang 'Nessun Dorma', with a guitar and a Russian hat; at the highest note, he stopped and turned to the coffin, putting his hand towards Malcolm to do the next bit – 'Come on, come on, Malcolm.' Everybody was laughing and clapping. I know this is not a conventional approach, and it may indeed seem disrespectful to some people, but this was just the way it had to be for Malcolm.

Then we approached the coffin for the final goodbye and commendation of the dead, to walk Malcolm from the church. We put our shoulders under the coffin and lifted it slowly to the strains of the old rock and roll hit 'Return to Sender'. Everybody started to sing and jive as we walked down the aisle with the coffin. The family, with smiles on their faces, looked at me trying to be my usual quite serious self, and I had to smile with them. Even I was singing as we were walking out with Malcolm, and I think they enjoyed the fact that I too was really taking part in the service.

It was a marvellous experience and I didn't miss a second of that service – it was incredible. It was like going to the London Palladium for a two-hour show – amazing! Then we left the church to a piper (not my favourite, as loyal readers will know), but this again added to the flavour of the day. Hundreds of balloons were released. After the cremation at Hither Green Crematorium, we took all the flowers and the family back to the wake at the Trafalgar Tavern, where, in true naval tradition, so I am told, a few of Malcolm's personal artefacts were auctioned off. Then all the flowers were thrown into the Thames at high tide, to more speeches and even more music. I am told that the wake went on into the early hours of the morning, and I am sure that Malcolm's friends and anybody who saw, touched or felt that funeral in any way will have it etched on their memory for time immemorial.

The poem below, 'Ode to a Great Father', written by Poppy Hardee, says it all. Malcolm was a most unusual father, one who was deeply loved and rewarded with all he had left behind.

Ode to a Great Father

Dad, many will remember you
As an entertainer and a man of wit,
Others as a showman and a general twit.

But not me.
Do you know what I see?

I see a man of compassion
Fighting never to be ignored,
A man who rarely made any of us bored.

ONE LAST ENCORE

If you had £10, you'd give it to someone in need,
No, scrap that, you'd bet it to make £20 in your desire to
Succeed.

You'd say you'd pick me up at two, yet arrive at four,
With a cheery 'oy oy' and a knock at my door.
But my anger would soon subside at one glance of your
   face,
But not at your attire,
your curry stained jackets and unzipped flies were a
   disgrace!

When I was with you, I'd laugh until I'd cry.
It doesn't seem quite right that you could leave us to die.
I don't believe in heaven but if I did
I know people would say you're up there not giving a shit.

But me, I don't agree.

You did give a shit and you certainly cared,
You'd hate it if people didn't notice you there.
You cared so deeply you'd give
Your whole world to see me happy,
Although according to Mum you never changed one of my
   nappies!

You've gone now and left a hole in my heart that may
   never be filled,

Strong Shoulders

For me, a part of my world is frozen and time stands still.

Wherever you go, wherever it may be,
I hope you'll bellow 'OY OY' and remember me!

Poppy Hardee xxx

p.s. You owe me 9 quid!

So there we have it – an incredible funeral. Yet, in my life, every funeral that I conduct is incredible in its own way, and every soul is as valued in my mind and actions.

So now I face the final curtain, as Frank Sinatra would say – well, the final curtain of writing about funerals, anyway. I hope you have enjoyed reading my books as much as I have enjoyed writing them, and if you haven't, well, you can't please everybody, can you? If, from writing any one of my books, I have left you a little less afraid of death and a little more focused on life and the life we all have left, I have succeeded. If I have made you think about death briefly and then put it to one side again, I have succeeded.

I hope too that we can all understand that laughter and tears are genuinely two sides of the same coin and can work in any situation. In my books, there have been many funny occasions and many sad occasions, occasionally moments of despair and, in some of the incidents I have recalled, moments of distastefulness and horror. All these put together are necessary in life and in death, and whatever the outcome of your reading my books, please believe me that I only ever meant to be constructive and helpful in what I wrote.

So what is the secret of my very limited success? Simple, I think. For me, it has been to be as good as I can be, however limited that might be at all times. I was not an early scholar, not a real boffin but a lazy boy at school. I picked up a lot at sixteen, and from that moment on I took every opportunity that life has offered me, every opportunity to learn every new skill possible, and I hope that my determination has taken me as far as I can go.

Unlike many others, unfortunately, I have tried to use every bit of my limited talent – even if I could not run as fast as the others in a race, I would at least run as fast as my legs would carry me, aiming to be as good as I could personally be. Some people have great talent but do not exploit it, do not make the best of themselves, but for me the only way to be a true champion in whatever field you are entering is to take all the talent you have and be the best you can be *every single day*. The best footballers in the world don't just have one good game every so often – they consistently perform at the highest level; that is what makes a champion. Nothing more, nothing less.

Perhaps only as a funeral director can I be some kind of mild champion. At least I have found my forte in life, my challenge, my ambition, my hopes and my prayers, all put together in one profession. And in whatever I do in life, at least people know I am there, and just being there is often enough. Remember that no one has to be alone, especially at times of bereavement: *Sic vos non solum vobis* – With us they are not alone.

The Funeral Director's Prayer

Lord, give me the patience needed to serve everyone
    as mine own;
The wisdom to understand others' feelings;
The knowledge to learn as well as to instruct;
The kindness to treat everyone equally at all times;
The strength to endure long hours and hard work;
The desire to serve others as I would my own family;
The humility to accept words of thanks and praise;
The compassion to touch another's soul;
The pride and the right to smile when I have served a
    family well;
And, Lord, most importantly the right to shed an
    honest tear when my heart is touched;
Lord, make me thankful that I am a Funeral Director.

(Anthony J. Asselta III)

WHEN SOMEONE DIES: HELPFUL HINTS AND MORE

The history of death and funerals in Britain

Victorian times to the birth of the National Health Service (1837–1948)
The prevalent image of the Victorian era is of the monarch dressed in full mourning unable to recover from the death of her husband Prince Albert in 1861. In the early part of Victoria's reign, some of her subjects did indeed emulate their sovereign's example through elaborate displays of grief, the writing of long eulogies on their loved ones' lives and photographs. Tombstones became important commemorative sites, well attended and maintained. Many early Victorians felt that closeness to the dead helped to perpetuate their memory.

Dominant though these images are, such attitudes to death were, however, relatively short-lived and not really typical of the period. The Victorians also did an enormous amount to reform funerals, starting with a series of Burial Acts in the 1850s, which established local Burial Boards with the power to raise money to fund cemeteries and close overcrowded and unhygienic churchyards. In addition, the British Undertakers' Association was formed in 1905.

From the 1870s, social and economic changes occurred that further altered attitudes to death. The Industrial Revolution was in full flow, leading to a better standard of living for many people, and the death rate declined rapidly, particularly among infants and young children. Within fifty years, death was seen more as a concern for the elderly, and society's preoccupation with dying began to decline.

This went hand in hand with a change in attitude to religion. Darwin first published his *Origin of Species* in 1859, and theories of evolution began to take hold. Attendance at church failed to keep pace with the growing population, and people started to question the Bible, with a growing band of people who did not believe in God at all. This decline in religious beliefs led to the rise of cremation as an alternative to burial. The Cremation Society was formed in 1874, arguing that cremation offered a more hygienic and economic alternative to burial. The first legal cremations took place in the 1880s, and the practice was enshrined in law through the 1902 Cremation Act. It was, however, slow in becoming popular as, even among unbelievers, many centuries of the Christian custom of burial were hard to shake off. It was not until 1944 that the Church of England officially accepted cremation, with the Vatican Council following in the 1960s (will freeze-drying and cryonics follow a similar road, I wonder?).

The two World Wars completely changed society's thinking and attitude towards death. Any vestiges of the early Victorian ways of mourning the dead were seen to be completely irrelevant in the face of so many young men in their prime dying violent deaths on foreign soil. A new way of mourning was required, and the country flocked to witness the interment of the Unknown Soldier in Westminster Abbey, representing all those who had died abroad, and united around public events such as Armistice Day and the Two Minute Silence.

The modern era (1948 onwards)

The establishment of the National Health Service (NHS) in 1948 had a profound effect on modern-day attitudes to death. The NHS cultivated and co-ordinated better public health measures, worked in partnership with the pharmaceutical industry to develop drugs, and advanced surgical treatments, all of which had a dramatic effect on life expectancy in Britain.

The introduction of the NHS also meant that more people than before died in hospital, which in turn affected the services that undertakers provided. When people died at home, undertakers provided the coffin and transportation, but with the rise in the number of hospital deaths, undertakers, or funeral directors as they were called from 1935, were required to offer a greater range of services, including chapels of rest, embalming, transport by car, cremation and refrigeration. Larger firms were able to offer all these services from one site and utilise greater economies of scale. Many of the independent companies that had previously been providing funeral services were bought out by larger firms, and today about one third of funeral directors are independent, the remainder being split between the Co-op and the corporation known as Dignity Funeral Services, both honourable public servants. In 1994, the government became involved in the regulation of funeral services and established the voluntary National Funeral Ombudsman scheme.

Throughout the latter half of the twentieth century, the public's knowledge of death and dying increased dramatically, and the Church no longer controlled people's understanding of death. Church doctrines offering consoling words and images were not just accepted without question, nor did the Church necessarily provide a ready-made supportive community following bereavement. A new need emerged that was filled by bereavement support groups and self-help networks, such as Cruse (now Cruse Bereavement Care) in 1959. These provided people with advice and the opportunity to speak to others about their experiences. The number of support groups has risen steadily during the past fifty years or so and today includes the funeral director in the front line.

Traditionally, Britons were expected to mourn behind closed doors and keep a stiff upper lip in public. However, the death of Diana, Princess of Wales, in 1997 turned many centuries of convention on its head. For three weeks the public flocked to Kensington Palace to lay flowers and other offerings in front of her former home, openly grieving for her loss. Since then the images of people publicly lamenting the death of loved ones have been regular media features.

Researching the local history of an area is often the best way of finding out more about the history of death and funerals in Britain. Churches and cathedrals often have interesting stories to tell. Look out for old tombstones, monuments and stained glass windows. Many local museums and attractions also have artefacts and excavations that tell you more about the history of how people were buried or cremated in that part of the country. Tourist Information Offices can provide details. Britain's changing attitudes to death are well documented in paintings and sculptures, so local and national art galleries showing historical work are also good sources.

The Bereavement Register

It is an inevitable consequence of our role as funeral directors that, every day, we come into contact with people at moments in their lives when they are at their most vulnerable. This is both a privilege and a responsibility as it affords us the opportunity to play a small role in guiding them through the trauma and confusion that always attends bereavement.

This confusion will inevitably extend beyond the strict confines of the funeral director's service and may include offering guidance on how to navigate the maze encountered by the immediate need to put in order at least some of the deceased's affairs. This is why any service or initiative that makes this process less stressful for the bereaved and which, in a sensitive and responsible manner, addresses the needs of the family during the weeks and months after bereavement is to be commended. It is why I, like many of my fellow funeral directors, support and commend the Bereavement Register to our clients.

There can be few more pertinent reminders of one's loss than the repeated receipt of unwanted direct mail addressed to a deceased loved one, particularly if the marketing messages contained therein – albeit unintentionally – speak of potentially distressing things such as enjoying the holiday of a lifetime with a partner. If you are somebody who has found this to be a problem, be assured that you are not alone. In fact, mailing the recently deceased remains the number one complaint received by the Information Commissioner, formerly the Data Protection Registrar.

The Bereavement Register, however, provides the bereaved with a free and completely confidential way in which to take control of the situation. By adding your deceased loved one's details to the Bereavement Register, you can ensure that many of the UK's leading direct mailers will remove their names from their mailing lists and effectively put an end to this insensitive communication.

There are two important facts you should know about the Bereavement Register. First, the information you provide is held in total confidence and is used purely for the purpose of screening mailing lists. No information – neither the details of the deceased nor the details of the people who register the deceased – are ever released for other purposes. Second, it works. The Bereavement Register is used to screen more than half the direct mail sent to consumers in the UK, and in 2004 it prevented more than twenty-two million pieces of direct mail from being sent to the deceased.

You will receive information and registration forms for the Bereavement Register as a matter of course from most Registrars when you register the death of your loved one, and from more than half of UK's 4,600 funeral directors. Alternatively, you can register online at www.the-bereavement-register.com

It is unlikely, given the multitude of emotions and issues that will confront you at the point of bereavement, that putting a stop to unwanted and potentially distressing direct mail will be a priority. However, in the weeks and months that follow, when you are adjusting to new normality, your ability to take control and end the nuisance of unwanted mail makes the Bereavement Register a welcome and highly valuable service.

What to do when someone dies

Knowing what practical steps to take when someone dies can help to steer you through the first shock and distress of losing a loved one.

At home
If the death occurs at home, call your doctor, the out-of-hours emergency doctor or, if you do not know these, the police. You also need to call a funeral director.

Your doctor will issue a medical certificate of the cause of death, although in certain circumstances he or she may want to refer the death to the local Coroner. If there is any doubt about whether the person is dead or it is an emergency situation, dial 999. In such cases, the paramedics can confirm the death and inform the doctor and Coroner.

The person who certifies the death or your funeral director will also give you the details of your nearest Registrar of Births, Deaths and Marriages and information about how to register a death.

Unless a doctor or Coroner gives permission, the funeral director should not remove the body until the death has been certified.

In a nursing home
When someone dies in a nursing home, the staff will inform the next of kin as soon as possible. They will also make arrangements for registering the death and provide details

of the nearest Registrar. They may also make arrangements for the deceased to be transferred to a local funeral director's chapel of rest. It is definitely worthwhile letting the nursing home know your preferred funeral director.

In hospital
If the death is expected, the hospital will issue the medical certificate of the cause of death and may organise for the body to be transferred to the hospital's mortuary. If the death occurs as the result of an emergency or during an operation, the local Coroner will be informed. Hospital staff will make arrangements with the next of kin for the deceased's belongings to be collected. Many hospitals have a member of staff whose job it is to help relatives make the first arrangements and advise them on bereavement support groups (these are often referred to as Bereavement Offices).

Abroad
When someone dies abroad or on a foreign aircraft or ship, the death has to be registered according to the laws of that country and the local authorities will issue a death certificate. Your tour guide, the local police or the British Consul (details can be found in guidebooks or obtained from tour operators, the local police or hotels) can help with this. The British Consul will also provide translation services and advise on registering the death in the UK.

261

Anyone reporting a death abroad needs to have the following information about the deceased and themselves:

- full name;
- date of birth;
- passport number;
- where and when the passport was issued;
- the next of kin of the deceased person.

Arrangements can be made for the funeral to be held locally or for the body to be transported back to the UK through an international funeral director like Albin's or its sister company, Kenyon Christopher Henley. Always make sure that your holiday insurance policies cover repatriation after death, as the cost of transporting a body can run into thousands of pounds. Insurance companies or international funeral directors can advise on bringing a body back home. To arrange a funeral back home you will need:

- an authenticated translation of the death certificate, stating the cause of death, from the country where the death occurred;
- a certificate of non-liability to register from the Registrar of the district where the funeral is to take place.

To organise a cremation, you will also need a cremation order form from the Home Office. Your funeral director should be able to arrange all these requirements. (In all cases, the Coroner should be informed and given sight of the relevant documents.)

The Coroner

If the death is sudden and unexpected or at all suspicious, the Coroner's Office may need to be involved. The police, a doctor or the hospital can refer a death to the Coroner's Office. The Coroner will then decide whether a post-mortem or inquest is needed and will keep the next of kin informed about what to do. If a post-mortem is requested by a Coroner, it is a legal requirement and the consent of relatives is not required. The Coroner of the area where the deceased is lying on return to the UK must be told and given sight of the documents. The Coroner will then allow you to continue with your funeral arrangements or will undertake a post-mortem and possible inquest. The Coroner will issue an order for burial or cremation once any investigations have been completed.

The Coroner is required to retain all tissues and organs for as long as the legal procedures require, which is in practice usually for as long as it takes to determine the cause of death.

In Scotland, there are no Coroners as such, the duties instead being carried out by the Procurator Fiscal.

Hospital post-mortems

Hospitals may carry out a post-mortem if doctors feel that it would reveal more about how the deceased died; it can sometimes also be held at the relatives' request. The consent of relatives is required beforehand. In these circumstances, you may withhold consent if you wish.

Pathologists determine the cause of death and may ask whether they can retain certain organs or tissues for medical research purposes or to educate students, for example. Permission is required from relatives before any organs can be retained. Hospitals have publications available that explain more about post-mortems.

Registering a death
In England and Wales and Northern Ireland, all deaths should be registered within five days if possible. The death must be registered by the Registrar of Births, Deaths and Marriages in the sub-district where it occurred. The Registrar's address can be found by looking in the phone book under 'Registration of Births, Deaths and Marriages' or obtained from the doctor, local council or police station. Find out when the Registrar is available as some operate an appointment system.

By law, only certain people (known as informants) are able to register a death. These are:

- a relative;
- someone who was present at the death;
- the occupier (for example, the owner of a nursing home or the warden of a block of flats) of the building where the death occurred;

- the person taking responsibility for organising the funeral;
- the executor or executrix.

If the death has been referred to the Coroner's Office, the Coroner will inform the Registrar.

The Registrar will ask for the following information about the deceased:

- date and place of death;
- full name (and maiden name if applicable);
- date and place of birth;
- occupation (and husband's occupation if applicable);
- usual address;
- whether the deceased was receiving a pension or other allowance from public funds;
- the names and occupations of both parents, if relating to a child under sixteen years of age.

The Registrar may ask to see the following paperwork if it is available:

- the medical certificate of the cause of death;
- the deceased's NHS card, birth and marriage certificates, if you can find them;
- any pension books;
- the 'pink form' (Form 100), if one has been supplied by the Coroner.

The Registrar will give the informant copies of the death certificate (the entry in the General Register), a certificate for burial or cremation (known as the 'green form') and a certificate of registration of death. The 'green form' needs to be given to the funeral director before the funeral can go ahead. The certificate of registration of death is for Social Security purposes; the questions on the back should, if applicable, be answered and the form returned to the local Social Security office.

You will need several copies of the death certificate, and it is as well to get the number of copies you require at the time of registering the death (the Registrar can advise here). There is a small charge for this service.

The laws about registering a death in Scotland are slightly different. Deaths must be registered within eight days, and Scottish Registrars issue a certificate of registration of death, which should be given to a funeral director, a registration or notification of the death certificate for Social Security purposes, and extracts of the entry in the register (for a fee).

Planning a funeral
Most people plan a funeral service with a funeral director, and there are several choices you need to make about the sort of funeral that you want for your loved one or to ensure that their wishes are carried out.

One of the first things you will be asked is whether you

want to see the deceased in the funeral director's chapel of rest or alternatively rest the deceased at home. Some people find that this helps them come to terms with the fact that their loved one has died, while others find the thought distressing. You have a completely free choice.

You will also be asked whether you want to include mementoes in the coffin. If your relative is being buried, there is no restriction on what you can place in the coffin, but with cremation mementoes have to be combustible – the funeral director can advise.

Embalming temporarily delays the decay of the body and can make the deceased look more like they did when they were alive. There may be an additional charge for this service, but if the deceased is to be viewed by family and friends or if the funeral takes place more than five days after death, it is definitely advisable.

Nowadays, a wide range of coffins is available, and your funeral director should be able to obtain them.

The funeral director or the family can appoint someone to officiate at the funeral. The family will meet this person to talk about the service, their loved one and the practicalities. The majority of funeral services are conducted by a religious minister, but this does not have to be so. The family should be consulted about the music played during the service and whether it will be recorded or live. There should also be opportunities for family and friends to make a speech about the deceased and/or read a meaningful passage from a religious or other text. Many families also choose to design their own funeral service programmes with information about the deceased and the order of service.

Deaths are often announced in local papers or national dailies, together with when and where the funeral is being held. It is increasingly common for donations to be made to a charity in memory of the deceased as well as, or instead of, flowers. The standard practice is for the funeral director to collect donated money on behalf of the charity and to receive any floral donations, but they can also be given directly.

If your loved one is being cremated, you need to make a decision about the ashes and let the authorities know. Ashes can be scattered or buried at crematoriums, or taken away by the relatives. Separate ceremonies can then be organised for the dispersal of the ashes, or for them to be buried in a churchyard or cemetery; at Albin's, they can be placed in the Cremation Cemetery Memorial Garden (ask your funeral director whether they have one too).

The most important thing about planning a funeral is that you are clear about what is going to happen on the day. Funerals are emotional events, so you do not want to be worried about the practicalities. Those involved in preparing and executing funerals are very used to answering relatives' queries and will not mind going over things several times if that is what you feel you need.

Choosing a funeral director

There are about 4,600 funeral directors in Britain so choosing one can be difficult. Hospitals, doctors or friends can sometimes supply a list of local firms and/or make recommendations. A personal recommendation is usually the best advice.

There is no compulsory training or regulation needed to become a funeral director so, as a client, it is worth being aware of your basic rights. At Albin's, for example, we have an in-house education programme, and every member of staff has a qualification from our internal college. If a funeral director is a member of a trade association, it means that they have agreed to comply with a code of practice set out by the organisation. It also means that, should things go wrong, you can contact the association for advice and support. Be sure to check directly with the association that the funeral company is a registered member rather than just taking the company's word for it.

Although there is no specific regulation pertaining to funeral directors, most reputable companies have agreed to:

- provide clear information about services and prices;
- produce a written estimate of funeral charges and a detailed funeral account;
- protect clients' confidentiality;
- tell clients how they can make a complaint.

Discuss the services you want fully with the funeral director and make sure that you receive an itemised written quotation.

Paying for a funeral
The average cost of a funeral can range from £1,500 to £2,500 so be clear about how you are going to pay for it. The funeral director should ask whether there is a problem with meeting the costs of the funeral and advise on sources of help and payment plans. You may also be able to get help with the costs if you are receiving one or more of the following:

- income support;
- income-based jobseeker's allowance;
- housing benefit;
- council tax benefit;
- working families' tax credit;
- disability working allowance.

To see whether you are eligible and to make a claim, get in touch with your local Social Security office; your funeral director will be able to help and advise. Your funeral director may also advise on filling in the forms and should help you to complete them. Any payment received may have to be paid back once the deceased's estate has been assessed – usually a few months after death if there is any value in the estate. If there is no money, the payment will not have to be repaid.

Funeral directors submit a bill shortly after the funeral service. The bill should be fully itemised so that you can see what you are paying for. Settle the account as soon as possible, as legally the funeral bill is the first claim on the deceased's estate.

Benefits
When a spouse, partner or close relative dies, you may be eligible for certain payments from the state. These can include help with funeral expenses, bereavement benefits, housing benefit, jobseeker's allowance and council tax benefit.

Each individual's circumstances are assessed, so get in touch with your local Social Security office. This is listed in the business pages of phone books under 'Social Security' or 'Benefits Agency'; alternatively, details can be obtained from the Department for Work and Pensions' website at www.dwp.gov.uk

It is worth noting that a widow or widower aged sixty years or under for a woman and sixty-five years or under for a man may be eligible for £2,000 as a one-off payment. If you have children below school-leaving age, you may be able to claim a widowed parent's allowance.

Pre-paid funerals
Pre-paid funerals are becoming increasingly popular with those who want to specify the arrangements they would prefer and to spare their relatives the cost. These plans can be covered in a lump sum or instalments.

Make sure that the funeral provider is registered with the Funeral Planning Council or the National Association for Pre-Paid Funeral Plans. Albin's have their own plans available.

Cremation or burial?

Cremation
There are about 240 crematoria in the UK and around 72 per cent of people who die are cremated.

Cremation requires the following documents:

- a medical certificate of the cause of death (issued by a doctor to the next of kin);
- a certificate of cremation or burial (the 'green form' issued by the Registrar);
- an application for cremation (Form A, supplied by the crematorium and completed by the next of kin);
- authorisation for the dispersal of the ashes (the reverse of Form A);
- Form B (supplied and completed by the doctor who attended the deceased in their last illness);
- Form C (the back of Form B completed by an independent doctor endorsing the information in Form B);
- Form F (signed by the medical referee at the crematorium endorsing the information contained in Forms B and C).

The fees charged by crematoria vary, although they should be clearly displayed. The standard charges will usually include fees for the medical referee, the use of the chapel (whether for a religious or non-religious service) and the minister or officiant. There also will be additional charges for the various forms of memorial available.

Crematoria operate strict appointment systems, most allowing thirty to forty-five minutes for each funeral service.

Burial

Burial space in the UK is at a premium, and most of the 1,124 cemeteries are almost full. Churchyards, particularly those owned by the Church of England, are also very full or even disused, with space only for the burial of urns.

Relatives of those choosing burial need to supply a certificate of cremation or burial (the 'green form' issued by the Registrar) and an application for burial (supplied by the funeral director). It is sometimes possible to purchase the rights to a particular plot of land in a cemetery in advance. If the deceased has done this, relatives must present the form (known as a deed of grant) with the other documents. Other cemeteries do not allow clients to purchase exclusive space, and in these circumstances graves will be dug deep enough to accommodate three or four burials in the same spot. There are usually regulations prohibiting further interments for a set number of years, commonly seven or fourteen.

Most cemeteries are non-denominational, although there are others set aside for specific religions. In non-denominational cemeteries, sections may be reserved for particular religions.

The fees for burial in a cemetery vary and may be requested in advance of the funeral.

Those wanting a churchyard burial should ask the local vicar, rector or priest whether there is any space and whether their application is likely to be accepted. The application needs to be sent to the Diocesan Registrar, who can grant a licence reserving a plot. The church will charge for burials.

Woodland and green burials

The number of woodland and green burials has grown in the past ten years, and there are now over 160 sites. These sites keep the environment as natural as possible. Instead of having gravestones, trees or flowers are planted as memorials, sometimes with a name plaque, and all materials used are biodegradable. A number of funeral directors now include green funerals in their range.

Cryonics

Cryonics is the process of freezing the body after death in the hope that future scientific developments will allow frozen people to be revived. Medical procedures are carried out, and the body is cooled to $-196°C$. The practice is very limited in the UK, although Albin's are certified to carry out the procedure. People frozen in the UK are then transported to the USA to the Cryonics Institute for storage. More information is available from the Cryonics Institute's website at www.cryonics.org

World religions and funerals

The Baha'i faith

The Baha'i faith is a comparatively young independent religion that began in Iran in the mid-nineteenth century. Baha'is follow the teachings of the Prophet Founder Baha'u'llah, who taught that there is only one God and that the fundamental purpose of religion is to promote unity and harmony. Baha'is believe in equal rights for men, women and children; the elimination of all forms of prejudice; economic justice; education for all; and that religion goes hand in hand with science.

The Baha'i faith teaches that the body is the spiritual temple so it should never be cremated but interred somewhere no more than one hour's journey away from the place of death. The body is wrapped in a shroud of white silk or cotton, and a ring bearing a specific inscription is placed on the deceased's finger. A coffin made of crystal, stone or hard, fine-quality wood is used. The family or Baha'i community will arrange for a specific Prayer for the Dead to be said before burial.

National Spiritual Assembly of the Baha'is of the
United Kingdom
27 Rutland Gate, London SW7 1PD
Tel: 020 7584 2566
Website: www.bahai.org.uk

Buddhism
The Buddha (which is a title meaning 'Awakened One')
was an Indian prince named Siddhartha Gautama who
lived two and a half centuries ago. Buddhists follow the
example he set in the way that he lived his life, and
endeavour to learn to do good, cease to do evil and purify
their own minds. Buddhism spread throughout the East
from India, taking on the particular traditions of the
countries that adopted it. There are three main schools of
Buddhism (Theravada, Mahayana and Vajrayana), each
with its own traditions. The school of Buddhism they
belong to and their country of origin determine the precise
customs and rituals followed by Buddhists.

Death is generally seen as an inevitable part of life. The
most important point is to avoid anything that will cause
the dying person's mind to become more disturbed than it
may already be. Although it is understood that those left
will naturally mourn, it is accepted that excessive grieving
helps neither the deceased nor the bereaved. It is thought
that the dead person's consciousness, or essence, remains
around the body for a time after death, so it can be assisted
or hindered by the behaviour of the bereaved. However, the

state of a person's mind approaching death is considered paramount as this is believed to influence the characteristics of their rebirth or reincarnation. Chanting or meditation may be used to achieve peaceful surroundings.

When a Buddhist dies a Buddhist monk or nun, ideally from the same school of Buddhism as the deceased, is informed as soon as possible; this person then initiates the particular rituals. Buddhists see the body as a shell of the spirit, so many prefer cremation, which usually takes place three to seven days after death.

The Buddhist Society
58 Eccleston Square, London SW1V 1PH
Tel: 020 7834 5858
Website: www.thebuddhistsociety.org

Christianity
Christians come from a broad variety of cultures, crossing all continents, and Christianity covers many different denominations. Broadly speaking, the Christian Church split into two branches during the Great Schism of 1054, forming the Eastern Orthodox (mainly Russian and Greek) and the Western Catholic Churches. The Western Church split again in the sixteenth century, and there are now many denominations, including Roman Catholic, Anglican, Baptist, Methodist, Quaker, Pentecostal and Presbyterian. In the twentieth century, the ecumenical movement has been gathering strength in an attempt to bring all the

different Christian denominations closer together.

Christians can be either buried or cremated, although some traditions retain a strong preference for burial. The funeral usually takes place four to ten days following death. The general tenor of funeral services is to give thanks for the deceased's life, pray for those who mourn and commend the deceased to God's everlasting mercy. Some funerals may take the form of a special celebration of the Eucharist (which recalls the Last Supper that Jesus Christ shared with his disciples before his death), often known as a Requiem Mass. Black has traditionally been worn to funerals, but many these days choose simply to wear dark colours, although some break from tradition and wear bright colours to celebrate life and resurrection.

Most Christian funerals now take place in the chapel of a cemetery or crematorium, although a significant number are held at the deceased's local church, with the coffin and mourners then travelling to the cemetery or crematorium for the final committal.

Funeral services may be followed by a later memorial service, which gives thanks for the person's life in a more public way with a wider group of friends and colleagues.

Churches Together in Britain and Ireland
Inter-Church House, 35–41 Lower Marsh, London
SE1 7SA
Tel: 020 7523 2121
Website: www.ctbi.org.uk

Hinduism

There is no single prophet or founder, or single holy book, so Hindus worship in a variety of ways, follow different customs and celebrate festivals as determined by their region of origin, family or original choice. However, all Hindus believe in Brahman, an all-encompassing oneness and a balanced way of living (physically, socially, ethically and spiritually).

Death represents the transition of the soul from one embodiment to the next. Hindus believe in reincarnation, and the state of a person's mind as they are dying is vital in determining the form of their reincarnation. A Hindu who is dying may read scriptures and hymns, and want to lie on the floor to be closer to Mother Earth. Another Hindu performs certain rites, and the family bring clothes and money for the dying person to touch. After death, the body is ritually washed, usually by the family. Adult Hindus are cremated as this signifies the release of the spirit, although infants and young children may be buried. The ashes are scattered in a flowing river, preferably the River Ganges.

Readings from the Holy Books take place for several days following the death. White is the traditional colour of mourning, and there is an official period of mourning of ten to thirteen days following the cremation, during which time the family remains indoors and friends visit to offer condolences.

For more information about the beliefs and teaching of Hindus, including links to numerous organisations round the world and regular news updates, log on to www.hindu.org General information about Hinduism, plus details of educational activities in schools, can be found at www.vivekananda.co.uk

Islam

The religion of Islam is based on revelations given to the Prophet Muhammad during the seventh century. Followers believe in the one and only God, known as Allah in the Arabic language, and that Muhammad is his final messenger. There are five pillars of Islam that underpin the practices of Muslims: the declaration of their faith, praying five times a day, fasting, giving a percentage of their income to charity, and making a once-in-a-lifetime pilgrimage to Makkah (Mecca).

For a Muslim, death is viewed as the start of real life – his or her eternal life. Dying Muslims may want to lie with their face towards the Muslim holy city of Makkah (south-east in the UK), and another Muslim may whisper the declaration of the faith to the dying person.

Muslims believe that the soul departs at the moment of death, and once someone has died their body is the property of God. The deceased is placed with their face towards Makkah. The body is ritually washed by family members, close friends or other Muslims, usually according to the gender of the deceased. Once it has been prepared, the body is wrapped in several shrouds of simple, white material and buried as soon as practical after death in the Muslim section of the cemetery – Muslims are never cremated.

Funerals are simple, respectful affairs, and mourning is allowed as long as it is not hysterical in nature. Muslims are generally buried facing Makkah in a grave marked with a simple tombstone.

The Muslim Council of Britain
Boardman House, 64 Broadway, Stratford, London E15 1NT
Tel: 020 8432 0585/6
Website: www.mcb.org.uk

Judaism
Observers of the Jewish faith believe in one universal God who handed down the Torah (the Holy Book containing the laws and commandments by which the Jewish people live) directly to Moses. Moses then passed these to the Jewish people. There is a wide spectrum of belief among Jews, ranging from Orthodox, Conservative and Reform, to Liberal and non-practising.

Jewish customs dictate that the deceased should be buried within twenty-four hours of death, although burial might be delayed by the Sabbath. Jewish communities have a Chevra Kadisha (burial society) that prepares the body for burial and helps to make the funeral arrangements. Funerals are generally simple affairs. Bodies are not embalmed as Jews believe that the soul ascends to Heaven as the body decays.

Starting from the day of the funeral, there is an official period of mourning lasting seven days (Shiva). Several mourning customs apply to the seven immediate members of the deceased's family (mother, father, son, daughter, brother, sister and husband or wife). They are not allowed to wear leather shoes, put on make-up, use perfume, shave, have a haircut or bathe. All mirrors in the family house also have to be covered during Shiva. Small symbolic tears are made in the chief mourners' clothes before the funeral service. During Shiva, other family members and friends visit to offer their condolences, usually bringing gifts of kosher food or fruit. Different Jewish communities then observe other customs throughout the year following death.

News, education, events and a Jewish community helpline are provided by:

The Board of Deputies of British Jews
6 Bloomsbury Square, London WC1A 2LP
Tel: 020 7543 5400
Website: www.bod.org.uk

Emotional help, support and information is offered to bereaved Jewish people by:

Jewish Bereavement Counselling Service
8/10 Forty Avenue, Wembley, London HA9 8JW
Tel: 020 8385 1874
Website: www.jvisit.org.uk/jbcs

Sikhism

The Sikh religion is based on the teachings of Guru Nanak, who was born in the Punjab, India, in the fifteenth century; nine other living Gurus followed, until the last in the line, Guru Gobind Sahib, would take over as the Guru for all Sikhs. The Holy Book of the Sikhs, the Guru Granth Sahib, is treated with the utmost respect and is central to Sikh customs, ceremonies and festivals. Sikhs believe in one God and the equality of all humanity. They believe that God is not exclusive to any one religion and that everyone should be free to follow his or her own faith.

Sikhs believe in an afterlife. When a Sikh is dying, relatives and friends read from the Guru Granth Sahib, especially the Psalm of Peace. At the point of death, no loud mourning is allowed. Instead, Sikhs chant, '*Waheguru, Waheguru*' (Wonderful Lord) and wash the deceased's body.

Sikhs are cremated following a laying-in period at the family home during which the body is on display. There is a Sikh custom that the eldest son and other male relatives are the last to touch the body. In modern crematoria, those family members usually press the button that sends the coffin down to the furnace.

The ashes of the dead are dispersed in the nearest running river. Family and friends read the entire Guru Granth Sahib during the mourning period, which lasts about ten days.

World Sikh Foundation
33 Wargrave Road, South Harrow
Middlesex HA2 8LL
Tel: 020 8864 9228

Further information about the main religions observed in Britain is available from:

The Inter Faith Network for the UK
8A Lower Grosvenor Place, London SW1W 0EN
Tel: 020 7931 7766
Website: www.interfaith.org.uk

Without prejudice, and with thanks to Ginger TV, Scottish Television and Albin's Funeral Directors. Thanks also to Natasha Roe for some of the writings.

A BERMONDSEY BOY

A little bit ooh, a little bit aah
But if you're a Bermondsey Boy you know who you are.

Ducking and diving to get through the day
That's not a crime it's the Bermondsey way.

Stick with ya friends through to the end
That's the real message a Bermondsey Boy sends.

Jobs in the City replaced jobs in the Docks
We think on our feet and no one gets knocked.

We remember the past, we care for our old
We can't be bought and we can't be sold.

Dapper and as sound as a pound
A Bermondsey Boy will never let you down.

We are proud of our heritage and sure of our friends
We're never tight, we love a good spend.

Bermondsey, Bermondsey I could never let you go
For you're in my heart and you're in my soul.

(Barry Dyer)

CLOSING REMARKS

If you are wondering what people think of being written about in my books, read on! This was by a family whose story was told in my last book, *Bury My Heart in Bermondsey* – remember the spooky chapel lights story?

Dear Barry,
I have just finished your third book (*Bury My Heart in Bermondsey*) and feel that I must write to you and say a massive 'thank you'.

   Not only did you and your staff provide an excellent, warm and friendly service to us when we needed it, you also did our mum proud by writing about her in your book.

   I needed to say thank you because not only does our mum live on in our hearts forever, she will now live on in the thoughts of many other people through your book.

Barry, you're amazing. [I wish!]
Thank you, Thank you, Thank you.

Joanne
X

No, thank *you*, Joanne: you're the amazing one.
Henry Wadsworth Longfellow wisely wrote:

Life is real! Life is earnest!
And the grave is not its goal:
Dust thou art, to dust returnest,
Was not spoken of the soul.

Remember all that is is for ever, especially the soul.

I make no apologies for the repetitions in my four books – some things are worth repeating again and again! I hope that you find *Final Departures* interesting and different, and that the trilogy of *Don't Drop the Coffin*, *Bury My Heart in Bermondsey* and *Strong Shoulders* truly represents a kind of plan for this world and the next, or at least a sample of how I have lived my life. For better or worse, it has been an interesting journey so far.

So, here is my philosophy (as I truly believe that you must have a plan for life and death). Live each moment for itself: whether good, bad or indifferent, it is still the moment you are living. Do not worry about what might never happen. Let the future worry about itself, for it will unfold in time as yet another moment we will live through – or not, as the case may be. Worry cannot change this; this thought in itself does not hold the key. You see, for every action there is a reaction. So let your reaction be without remorse; let it depict your plan for life, a plan that, I hope, can accept death with respect yet with a little less fear, although fear will naturally always be present.

I hope I have reflected all this in the trilogy, as that was sincerely my aim. Read together, they represent my work, my life and my acceptance of death as a natural part of our existence, even though it is from our first breath our common enemy and is yet, I believe, also our final peace. For life itself is a truly precious gift. Enjoy it – it's not a rehearsal. Live long, be happy, and don't waste a moment (take it from an undertaker). The End (I think).

Barry
2005

Janua vitae
Death is the gateway to everlasting life

APPENDIX

LAST WILL & TESTAMENT FORM

This is
The Last Will & Testament

of me

of

in the County of   LONDON   made this day

I hearby revoke all Wills and Codicils made by me at any time heretobefore. I appoint

to be my executor/executrix and direct that all my debts and Funeral Expenses shall be paid as soon as conveniently may be after my demise.

I hearby give and bequeath

Signed by the said Testator, in the presence of us, present at the same time who at his/her request in his/her presence, and in the presence of each other have subscribed our names as witnesses on this day :

_____

_____

_____